TURNINGPOINTS

Preeminent writers offering fresh, personal
perspectives on the defining events of our time

Published Titles

William Least Heat-Moon, *Columbus in the Americas*

Scott Simon, *Jackie Robinson and
the Integration of Baseball*

Alan Dershowitz, *America Declares Independence*

Thomas Fleming, *The Louisiana Purchase*

Eleanor Clift, *Founding Sisters and
the Nineteenth Amendment*

William F. Buckley, Jr., *The Fall of the Berlin Wall*

Martin Goldsmith, *The Beatles Come to America*

Bob Edwards, *Edward R. Murrow and
the Birth of Broadcast Journalism*

Forthcoming Titles

Douglas Brinkley on the March on Washington

Kweisi Mfume on Abraham Lincoln and
the Emancipation Proclamation

D-Day

Also by Martin Gilbert

D-Day

MARTIN GILBERT

WILEY

John Wiley & Sons, Inc.

Published by John Wiley & Sons, Inc., Hoboken, New Jersey
Published simultaneously in Canada

Design and production by Navta Associates, Inc.

For general information about our other products and services, please contact our Customer Care Department within the United States at (800) 762-2974, outside the United States at (317) 572-3993 or fax (317) 572-4002.

Wiley also publishes its books in a variety of electronic formats. Some content that appears in print may not be available in electronic books. For more information about Wiley products, visit our web site at www.wiley.com.

Library of Congress Cataloging-in-Publication Data:

Gilbert, Martin, date.
  D-Day / Sir Martin Gilbert.
      p. cm. — (Turning points)
Includes bibliographical references and index.
  ISBN 0-471-42340-8 (alk. paper)
  1. World War, 1939–1945—Campaigns—France—Normandy. 2. Normandy (France)—History, Military—20th century. I. Title. II. Turning points (John Wiley & Sons)
D756.5.N6 G58 2004
940.54'2142—dc22

                                                    2003023858

Printed in the United States of America

10 9 8 7 6 5 4 3 2 1

Contents

Preface

The Allied landings in 1944 might have ended in disaster. Winston Churchill thought he would be woken up to be told of massive casualties. General Eisenhower prepared a short, solemn broadcast announcing that the enterprise had failed.

D-Day in military parlance is the starting "day" of any offensive. In 1943 there had been both a Sicily D-Day and an Italy D-Day before the cross-Channel assault. But because the Normandy landings on 6 June 1944 marked so significant a turning point in the Second World War, the term "D-Day" has come to signify that day alone. My aim in these pages is to show how that turning point in history came about. The period of preparation, lasting almost two years—amid the strains and uncertainties of war elsewhere—was one of inventiveness, hard work, experimentation, secrecy, and wide-ranging deception plans.

This was no chance or accidental turning point, but a calculated, planned, evolving, intricate struggle to ensure the overthrow of a tyrannical regime, and to liberate those who had suffered under its harsh rule for four years. It was a struggle that involved men and women in offices and factories, in training camps and clandestine venues—almost none of them knowing the specific destination—working as a vast team to put together a comprehensive plan that would ensure the destruction of Hitler and his regime and the liberation of the captive peoples of Europe.

The turning point of 6 June 1944 owed its evolution and impact to many individuals and groups of individuals. Among them were the two statesmen, the British Prime Minister Winston Churchill and the American President Franklin D. Roosevelt, whose joint vision it was, despite disagreements and hesitations along the way; to General George C. Marshall and General Sir Alan Brooke, the respective heads of the vast American and British military organizations, who worked for it at the highest level of strategic planning; to General Dwight D. Eisenhower and General Bernard Montgomery, the American Supreme Commander and the British Commander-in-Chief, respectively, who had to carry out the strategy and work together in tandem. There were also the two staffs of both these commanders, men and women who had to coordinate a hundred different enterprises, and to the special organizations within those staffs, working to devise a successful amphibious landing on a scale never before attempted.

Others without whom the whole vast enterprise could not have been launched were the intelligence chiefs who masterminded the sending of Allied agents into Europe, and who controlled the double agents in Britain through whom the essential deception plans were promoted. Then there were the factory workers and engineers and builders and technicians and inventors who made the wide array of equipment needed. Much was also owed to the pilots and aircrews who were in action long before D-Day, on the day itself, and after it, helping to ensure success; to the sailors who cleared the seas and transported the invasion force and kept it supplied; and above all to the soldiers of all Allied armies, all ranks, and all branches of the armed services, who trained for action, and then went into action on the beaches and landing grounds of Normandy, and then fought their way across the Continent. It was a collective effort on an unprecedented scale. Without that effort the turning point would have been impossible.

Those who planned for a successful turning point had two unexpected advantages, one of which was beyond their control, the other of which they engineered. These were both mistakes made by their enemy. Hitler's decision to declare war on the United States, six months after he had invaded the Soviet Union, ensured that he had to confront a second powerful adversary before he had defeated the first. The Normandy landings would not have been possible without the substantial participation of the United States. Hitler's second mistake was carefully encouraged by the Allies: his belief that the real destination of the Allied forces—even after the landings had been made on the Normandy coast—was elsewhere, at the Pas-de-Calais. But the possibility always remained, until after the actual landings, that if the Germans decided to bring their maximum forces to bear on the beachhead, the Allied armies could be defeated on the shore.

Despite the enormous energy and ingenuity that went into the planning for D-Day, and despite the successful deception, the specter of failure was always present. Indeed, the debate over whether this was the best way to challenge the Nazi domination of Europe had been a long and divisive one. Even Churchill, who, in both the earliest and later stages was to be a strong advocate of the landings, had his doubts. As he later wrote: "I was not convinced that this was the only way of winning the war." Even after the decision to embark on a cross-Channel landing had been made, he had pressed for different military initiatives.

A failed Allied landing would not only have been a setback, it could also have been a disaster for the Allied cause. Hitler's regime would have seen an opportunity to regain the ascendant, and it possessed the means to do so. New, terrifying flying bombs and the even more powerful rocket bombs—with their one-ton warheads—were almost ready to be launched. Long-distance submarines were in the final stage of development, and these would enable Hitler's naval power to reach the eastern seaboard of the United States without having to refuel at sea. In addition, a mine against which there was no known defense was in the final stages of preparation: the first examples were actually used on D-Day.

Relieved from the need to fight an Allied army in the West, an enormous quantity of planes, tanks, troops, and armaments—a third of Germany's first-class fighting forces—would have been available to meet the Soviet eastern offensive, which had been planned by the Allies to follow the Normandy landings. The last remaining Jews of Europe—more than a million—were listed for deportation and death; the collaborators, trains, and gas chambers would have been available to seek them out and deport them, to internment and their deaths.

Failure at Normandy could have given Hitler—whose armies and Gestapo were in occupation or control from the Atlantic coast of France to the Polish-Soviet borderlands— the prospect of victory. The Soviet Union, after three years of war, was still fighting the German forces on its own soil, and still bleeding and burning on its own territory. Britain did not have the resources for a second amphibious assault without the United States. If the American armies had been forced to leave Normandy bloodied and defeated, the United States might well have decided—after two and a half years of focusing on the war in North Africa and Europe— to turn its main energies to the ever-growing demands of the war in the Pacific, and Europe would have been left to its own devices. Had that happened, I doubt that I—a seven-year-old British schoolboy at the time of the land-ings—would be alive to write this book, or free to express my opinions without fear of imprisonment—or death.

Sir Martin Gilbert
Honorary Fellow,
Merton College,
Oxford
25 November 2003

Acknowledgments

My first thanks are to the schoolmasters of Highgate School, who, in 1950, took a school group to the Normandy beaches. Signs of the landings were much in evidence then, as was the Allied destruction of Caen. In 1969 I made the first of several visits to Field Marshal Montgomery, who gave me an inscribed copy of his book *Normandy to the Baltic,* showed me his command caravans, and encouraged me in my work.

On my own subsequent visits to Normandy, most recently with a group of friends in 2003, I have benefited from the exceptional work done by Winston Ramsey, the editor of the two-volume *D-Day Then and Now,* and by Major and Mrs. Holt's most informative *Battlefield Guide to the Normandy Landing Beaches;* their respective volumes are an indispensable preliminary to any visit to or study of the Normandy landings. These, and many other historical works on which I have drawn, and without which no history of the Normandy landings could be written, are listed in the bibliography. I am also grateful to those who have sent me material or answered my queries, in particular Major Robert de L. Cazenove, Gunner Connell, Sue Ann Dunford, Lady

Dunluce, Suzan E. Hagstrom, Benjamin Meirtchak, Esther Poznansky, Sir Harry Solomon, Professor George J. Winter, and Morley Wolfe Q.C.

Michael A. Accordino, a veteran of the Normandy landings, sent me his typescript "Memoirs of a Soldier." James H. Burke sent me his recollections, compiled primarily as a record for his family "and its future descendants." Charles Delworth gave me his recollections of D-Day, as seen by an Allied soldier in Italy. John E. Dunford set out for me his personal account of the Normandy landings, as did Alf Freeman. Professor M. R. D. Foot gave me his personal recollections of the British parachute deception that drew German troops away from the American landing on Omaha Beach. Melvyn Greene, O.B.E., a British schoolboy at the time of D-Day, gave me a copy of his unpublished recollections, "A Boy's Memories alongside World Events." Judith Kramer gave me access to the diary of her father, Abe Kramer. Sir John Keegan gave me permission to quote from his own schoolboy recollections in his book *Six Armies in Normandy*. Tom Rice gave me access to his own memories, and those of his company officer Eugene D. Brierre, of parachuting on D-Day. Irving Rosenbluth recalled June 5 on an air base in Britain. Eugene D. Shales gave me his account, written for his grandchildren, of coming ashore on D-Day.

Max Arthur read the text with a knowledgeable eye. Erica Hunningher, Rima Weinberg Dudko, and Kimberly Monroe-Hill gave me the benefit of their expert editorial skills. Tim Aspden has transformed my rough draft maps into his usual high standard of clarity and presentation. Kay Thomson assisted with the substantial task of correspondence and organization, and also read the text.

Maps

Maps begin on page 182.

1

The Genesis of
a Plan

From the moment France was overrun by the German army in June 1940, it was clear that Germany could only be driven out of its western European conquests by a cross-Channel assault. It was also clear that British soil, which at its closest point was visible from the coast of German-occupied France, would have to be the launching ground. Following the Dunkirk evacuation, when 338,226 British, French, and other Allied troops had been evacuated, Hitler's military strength offered him the prospect of the mastery of Europe. To challenge that mastery a much larger army would be needed to cross back over the Channel.

Britain's military resources by themselves could never be sufficient for such a return in the strength needed to offer any prospect of success. Only if the United States, with its potential air, land, and naval strength—including landing craft—were to enter the war, would a return to Europe be possible. But even while substantially assisting Britain's war effort, America remained neutral throughout 1940 and until early December 1941.

Determined to find a means of launching a cross-Channel attack, Churchill—who had told the British people after Dunkirk, "Wars are not won by evacuations"—ordered the design and construction of landing craft. On 6 June 1940, only four days after the final evacuations from Dunkirk, he asked his defense staff to put forward "Proposals for transporting and landing tanks on the beach, observing that we are supposed to have command of the sea, while the enemy have not." On June 22, his mind still on a return to Europe, he wrote again to his defense staff: "We ought to have a corps of at least 5,000 parachute troops. I hear something is being done already to form such a corps, but only, I believe, on a small scale."

That day the British War Cabinet approved Churchill's proposal to establish the Special Operations Executive, known as SOE. Its purpose was sabotage, subversion, brief cross-Channel raids, and the creation of a secret force of agents behind the lines. Churchill set out the aim of this new body in three words: "Set Europe Ablaze!" Clandestine guerrilla operations would harass an occupying power and, when the moment came, assist an invading force.

On the day after the War Cabinet gave its approval to SOE, Churchill outlined its tasks. "It is of course urgent and indispensable," he wrote to a member of the War Cabinet, "that every effort should be made to obtain secretly the best possible information about the German forces in the various countries overrun, and to establish intimate contacts with local people, and to plant agents. This, I hope, is being done on the largest scale, as opportunity serves. . . ."

What Churchill had in mind was a series of raids of "not less than five nor more than ten thousand men," two or three of which raids he thought could be carried out against the French coast during the coming winter. "After these medium raids have had their chance, there will be no objection to stirring up the French coast by minor forays." These were to be followed during the spring and summer of 1941 by "large armoured irruptions."

To plan for future amphibious operations, on 15 October 1940, the Combined Operations Training Centre was established at Inveraray in Scotland, to provide training for embarkation, disembarkation, and landing under fire. A second component of the cross-Channel invasion was airborne attack by paratroopers. The first British paratroop operation, Operation Colossus, took place inside Italy on 14 February 1941, when thirty-five men were dropped on a sabotage mission to blow up a railway viaduct in the Apennines. The sabotage was successful, but the commandos were captured. Their colleagues continued to perfect their skills. On March 4, two commando units, each of 250 men, supported by two Royal Engineer demolition detachments, landed on the Lofoten Islands, off the northwestern coast of Norway, as part of an operation to seize an Enigma machine and codebook. The Enigma machine was the top-secret method of radio communication between the German High Command and the commanders-in-chief on land, at sea, and in the air.

The Lofoten Islands operation was successful, its secrecy maintained by the deception of a raid to destroy the local fish-oil factories and all available German shipping.

The first substantial SOE operation on mainland Europe was launched in March 1941, when its agents were parachuted into France, near Vannes, on the Bay of Biscay, to ambush two buses carrying German aircrews on their nightly journey to a German air base used for bombing raids against Britain. Unfortunately for the plan, between its preparation and execution the Germans tightened their security arrangements for the transfer of men to the airfield, and the mission had to be abandoned. It did, however, bring back to London valuable information about the situation in France.

Other operations followed: acts of sabotage, the establishing of SOE circuits inside France, contact with the French Resistance, and help for the Resistance in its own sabotage activities. It was clear, however, that the main task of these Resistance networks and their SOE helpers would come when the Allies were ready to make a major amphibious landing. In all, SOE established eighty-three circuits—groups of agents operating with the French Resistance—in France between the summer of 1941 and the Normandy landings three years later. Of these eighty-three circuits, thirty-three were destroyed by the Germans, some as a result of betrayal, others as a result of mischance. But fifty circuits were still functioning on the day of the cross-Channel landings. Of the 393 agents who worked in France, 119 were executed by the Gestapo or killed while carrying out their duties. Several thousand French men and women were also executed for their part in helping these circuits.

Hitler's European conquests continued throughout 1941. Greece and Yugoslavia were overrun that April, and in June the German onslaught turned against the Soviet Union. From the first months of the German attack, which penetrated deep into Russia, Britain gave massive help to the Soviet forces in the form of weapons, tanks, aircraft, munitions, medical supplies, and Intelligence information, making an important contribution to Russia's ability to continue to resist the German onslaught.

Britain also launched a number of commando raids in the West. On 27 July 1941 there was a small hit-and-run raid on the French coast near Ambleteuse, by an officer and sixteen men of No. 12 Commando.

On September 27 there was a further hit-and-run raid near the French seaside town of Luc-sur-Mer, which was later to be at the center of the Normandy landings. It was carried out by men of No. 1 Commando, who managed to cross the seawall, but were then met by machine gun fire and withdrew. Two commandos were taken prisoner, and one was wounded.

Within a month of this commando raid against the Normandy coast, Churchill instructed the newly appointed Commodore of Combined Operations, Vice Admiral Lord Louis Mountbatten, and his Combined Operations staff, to make plans for "our great counterinvasion of Europe." Churchill told Mountbatten: "The South Coast of England is a bastion of defence against Hitler's invasion; you must turn it into a springboard to launch an attack."

A raid on the French coast at Houlgate on November 23 was carried out by eighty-eight men of No. 9 Commando. It failed in its hit-and-run objective but taught Mountbatten "that the vital lesson of establishing and maintaining communications between shore and ship had not been learned." The learning was begun in earnest.

On 7 December 1941 Japan struck at Pearl Harbor. The American government and people were suddenly embroiled in war in the Pacific. Four days later, Hitler declared war on the United States. In Europe the work of the British commandos continued. On December 27 they carried out their largest raid thus far, when 51 officers and 525 men secured the temporary occupation of the port of South Vaagso, on the coast of central Norway, a crucial German shipping anchorage and coastal transit point. Men of No. 2, No. 3, No. 4 and No. 6 Commando took part, with considerable British naval and air forces participating, including a cruiser and four destroyers. The troops were put ashore in two lightly armored infantry assault ships (LCAs—Landing Craft, Assault), which had earlier been Belgian cross-Channel steamers.

A special unit of correspondents, photographers, and cameramen was also landed at Vaagso, to witness and report as German coastal defenses were demolished and 16,000 tons of German shipping destroyed. Before the German defenders were overrun, twenty of the raiding force were killed. Ninety-eight Germans were taken prisoner. Hitler concluded, "Norway is the zone of destiny in this war," and ordered substantial reinforcements. This gave the Allies a clear indication of where their future deception plans could be used to good effect.

In Washington, General Dwight D. Eisenhower, recently appointed a member of the War Plans Division of the War Department, and confronted during his first weeks with the division by the Japanese onslaught in the Pacific, felt that it was in the Pacific that the power of the United States should be concentrated. "I've been insisting Far East is central," he wrote on 1 January 1942, "and no other side shows should be undertaken until air and ground are in satisfactory state." With the grave situation of the Americans, British, and Dutch in the Far East, Eisenhower opposed two recently agreed-on Anglo-American projects: Operation

Magnet, the dispatch of American troops to Britain; and Operation Gymnast, a proposed Anglo-American assault on Vichy France in North Africa.

Three weeks later, as the Japanese stood ready to defeat the British in Malaya and the Americans in the Philippines, Eisenhower came around to the view that was beginning to prevail in Washington, and that he—in due course—was so massively to enhance. "We've got to go to Europe and fight," he wrote, "and we've got to quit wasting our resources all over the world—and still worse—wasting time." Eisenhower added: "If we're to keep Russia in, save the Middle East, India and Burma, we've got to begin slugging with air at western Europe; to be followed with a land attack as soon as possible."

Within a month of Hitler's declaration of war on the United States, Churchill traveled to Washington to see President Roosevelt, to secure an American commitment to the defeat of Germany in Europe before the defeat of Japan. His views fell on fertile ground. In the autumn of 1941 one of the leading American strategic thinkers, General Albert C. Wedemeyer, a staff officer in the War Department in Washington—who, as a captain, had spent three years before the war at the German staff college in Berlin—had presented a "Victory Plan" that stressed the massive mobilization of resources and manpower that would be needed to defeat Germany in the event of war. "Our principal theater of war is Central Europe," he wrote; Africa, the Near East, Spain, Scandinavia, and the Far East would be "subsidiary theaters."

At the Washington conference in December 1941, code-named Arcadia, Roosevelt, Churchill, and their military staffs agreed, as a basis of Anglo-American strategy, that "only the minimum forces necessary for the safeguarding of vital interests in other theaters should be diverted from operations against Germany." Following this guideline, and adopting the central theme of General Wedemeyer's earlier plan, on 20 February 1942 General Eisenhower, recently appointed Director of the War Plans Division, confirmed his support for "offensive operations" in the European Theater "and concurrently defensive operations in all others."

2

Adversaries and Allies

On 26 January 1942 the first American servicemen arrived in Britain. This was Operation Bolero. The transit of these troops across the Atlantic was an essential preliminary to any cross-Channel landing. The question of the actual date by which that landing would be possible was under active discussion that month between the British and American military, naval, and air chiefs. Germany's victories against Russia made it essential to find a way to stop Russia from being defeated. The summer of 1942 was considered by the Allied planners as the earliest possible date for a cross-Channel assault with any chance of success, perhaps in securing a permanent foothold on the Cotentin Peninsula, or in Brittany. Churchill strongly favored such action.

British commando raids against the French coast continued, including the first British wartime airborne operation into France. On the night of 27–28 February 1942 a raid was made at Bruneval, near Le Havre, to seize a German radar installation used to control the German night fighters opposing the Allied bomber offensive against Germany. Among those taking part were paratroops of the British 1st Airborne Division. The radar equipment was dismantled and taken back to Britain.

From Moscow, Stalin was calling for a Second Front as soon as possible. He wanted an Allied landing in the summer of 1942—in two or three months' time. Hitler could not know when any such attempt would be made, but sensing that it must come sooner or later he was taking steps to deal with a possible Allied assault in the West. His plan was for a defensive barrier—known as the Atlantic Wall— from the Atlantic coast of Norway to the French border with neutral Spain in the Bay of Biscay. It was to consist of 15,000 fortified concrete bunkers built at fifty to a hundred yard intervals. In March 1942 Field Marshal von Rundstedt was appointed to command Army Group West (Commander-in-Chief West). He at once gave orders to incorporate the heavy gun emplacements at Calais—which had been erected as part of Germany's plans to invade Britain—into the new defensive structure.

On March 23 Hitler issued Führer Directive No. 40, Command Organization on the Coasts. In this he declared: "The preparation and execution of defensive operations must unequivocably and unreservably be concentrated in the hands of one man." This was a wise decision, but the complexity of the German command structure meant that it was never carried out—to the ultimate benefit of the Allies. Instead of a unified control, orders could be received by the troops in the field from three separate sources. The first was the commander of Army Group B, responsible for the defense of the area from Holland to the Atlantic coast of France (from February 1944 this command was held by

Field Marshal Rommel). The second was the Commander-in-Chief, West, Field Marshal von Rundstedt. The third was Hitler himself. Von Rundstedt was never able to obtain operational authority over either the German Air Force or the Navy.

Neither Stalin's needs nor Churchill's wishes for a cross-Channel operation in 1942 could be met. The blow came from Washington, which alone had the military man-power, and the airpower, sufficient to enable any cross-Channel landing to take place. On 7 March 1942, a black day for the "Second Front Now" campaign, Roosevelt informed Churchill, in strictest secrecy, that as a result of demands in the Pacific war zones, the American contribu-tion to land operations on the continent of Europe in the summer of 1942, the earliest possible date for some form of cross-Channel assault, would be "materially reduced." That is to say, the landings would have to be postponed.

Roosevelt warned Churchill that the shipping then avail-able to the United States would allow only 130,000 troops to be transported across the Atlantic by June 1942. Even with new United States naval construction, a vast increase on what had come before, no more than 170,000 American troops could be brought across by June 1943, and a total of 270,000 by December 1943. These were decisive facts: in his March telegram, Roosevelt stated that the earliest possible date by which the "troop-carrying capacity" of the United States could reach 400,000, the minimum figure then envis-aged for a major amphibious landing, was June 1944.

The facts set out in Roosevelt's telegram were a blow, to both Churchill and Stalin. But they represented the real-ity of the situation. Neither the Second Front—Stalin's succor—nor Hitler's defeat were imminent, or even near. But at the War Plans Division in Washington, Eisenhower was still an advocate of serious military action in northern Europe. On March 9, after speaking to General McNaughton, commander of the Canadian forces then in Britain, Eisenhower wrote: "—he believes in attacking in Europe. Thank God!"

Eisenhower's work had become crucial in the direction of American strategy. On March 25—two days after Hitler's order for a unified defense structure to meet an invasion—Eisenhower submitted his plan of future action to General George C. Marshall, the United States Army Chief of Staff, who presented it to Roosevelt that same day. The President was impressed, so much so that Eisenhower was asked to elaborate on the paper so that General Marshall could take it to Britain to present to Churchill and the British Chiefs of Staff.

Eisenhower's plan became known as the Marshall Memorandum. It proposed two possible amphibious operations. The first, code-named Round-up, was a full-scale amphibious cross-Channel landing, to be carried out on 1 April 1943. It envisaged a massive buildup of troops in Britain, far greater than previously believed possible. Thirty American and eighteen British divisions—almost 1,500,000 men—would be landed on the coast of northern France between Le Havre and Boulogne and advance on Antwerp. Seven thousand landing craft—they had not yet been built—would put the men on shore.

The second amphibious operation, to be launched no later than autumn 1942, would take place only if the Soviet Union was in danger of defeat, or if Germany's own military situation was "critically weakened." This was a much less ambitious, emergency plan, code-named Sledgehammer, an assault against Cherbourg, Brest, or both. Five British and five American divisions—some 330,000 men—would take part. These would include the 170,000 American troops whom Roosevelt had told Churchill could be available by June 1943.

Between April 10 and 14, in London, General Marshall and General Wedemeyer, accompanied by Roosevelt's personal emissary Harry Hopkins, presented Round-up and Sledgehammer to the three men whose support was essential: the Chief of the Imperial General Staff, General Sir Alan Brooke; Vice Admiral Lord Louis Mountbatten; and Churchill. Some caveats were put forward. With regard to Round-up, Brooke felt that the Japanese victories in the Pacific might force the Allies to concentrate their main military effort on the defense of India and the Middle East. With regard to Sledgehammer, he pointed out that only nine, not ten divisions would be available for such a landing by the autumn, and that the Germans would have overwhelming military superiority.

Mountbatten stressed, with regard to both operations, that the Allies did not have the number of landing craft needed. These were serious criticisms, but they could not override the imperative need for a plan of action. Britain and the United States would march together, Churchill told Marshall, "in a noble brotherhood of arms"; and to Roosevelt, Churchill telegraphed that "our agreed programme is a crescendo of activity on the Continent."

In Washington, at the War Plans Division, Eisenhower was relieved. "I hope that—at long last and after months of struggle by this division—we are all definitely committed to one concept of fighting." Neither Round-up nor Sledgehammer were to come to pass; but in them lay the genesis of the very landings that Eisenhower was in due course to command. In the United States, from the Great Lakes to the Gulf of Mexico, and along the eastern seaboard, a veritable armada of landing craft was even then under construction that would make those landings possible. (See the map on page 183.)

In London, on May 15, the first meeting was held of the Combined Commanders: senior British naval, air, and army chiefs whose task was to prepare an outline for military operations on the continent of Europe, and to make proposals for the detailed, complex, wide-ranging work that would have to be put in hand. They were joined within six weeks by General Eisenhower, who on June 24 was appointed Commanding General, European Theater of Operations, United States Army (ETOUSA), a post he was to hold until sent to North Africa at the end of 1942 to command the Allied forces there.

Stalin, whose forces were being hard-pressed by Hitler's armies for the second summer in succession, continued to demand a cross-Channel landing during the summer of 1942. On June 20, in New York, Churchill discussed this urgent appeal with Roosevelt. According to Roosevelt's advisers, the United States could provide only 700 of the 5,700 combat aircraft then judged necessary to secure air mastery over the landing beaches. With the full backing of the British Chiefs of Staff, Churchill told the President that "no responsible British military authority" could see any chance for a cross-Channel landing later that year.

Receiving daily reports of the fierce fighting and heavy casualties on the Eastern Front, Stalin continued to press that a Second Front be opened without delay. To explain the Anglo-American position to him, Churchill flew to

Moscow, accompanied by Roosevelt's emissary Averell Harriman. They would present Stalin with a united Anglo-American position.

At a meeting with Stalin on the evening of August 3, Stalin handed Churchill a document denouncing the British decision not to launch a cross-Channel attack in 1942. This decision, the document declared, "inflicts a mortal blow to the whole of Soviet public opinion" and "complicates the situation of the Red Army at the front and prejudices the plan of the Soviet Command."

According to the Soviet protest, the "most favourable" conditions existed for the creation of a second front in Europe in 1942, "inasmuch as almost all the forces of the German army, and the best forces to boot have been withdrawn to the Eastern front, leaving in Europe an inconsiderable amount of forces and these of inferior quality."

Churchill then repeated his arguments against a cross-Channel landing in 1942. "It would be no help to Russia," he said, "if the United Nations were to do something that would lead simply to disaster involving them in profitless loss." When Harriman declared, in support of Churchill, that "the President was prepared for any sacrifice which offered a reasonable prospect of success," Stalin replied that "if, as he assumed, Mr. Harriman was speaking of the 'torch' project, this operation did not concern the Soviet directly."

Torch was the code name for the operation favored by Britain and the United States: an amphibious landing in force on the Vichy French coast of North Africa, to secure Morocco for the Allies. As far as the second front was concerned, Stalin replied with bitterness that there was "a difference of view as to the importance of the Russian front." The Eastern Front, Stalin insisted, "was of first-rate importance, while he understood the British and American governments held it to be only of secondary importance." Hearing these angry words, Churchill "protested that this was not the case."

Churchill and his advisers prepared an answer to the Soviet document. It was a strong assertion that "the best front in 1942 and the only large-scale operation possible from the Atlantic is Torch." If this could be effected in October 1942, Stalin was told, "it will give more aid to Russia than any other plan." It also "prepares the way" for some further assault in 1943. But a cross-Channel attack on Cherbourg and the Channel Islands, Stalin was warned, "would be a hazardous and futile operation," that in the opinion of all British naval, military, and air authorities "could only end in disaster."

Even if such a landing itself took place successfully, "it would not bring a single division back from Russia," and would serve far more as "a running sore for us than for the enemy," using up "wastefully and wantonly the key men and the landing craft required for real action in 1943." That, the British stated, "is our settled view." Stalin, expressing admiration for the North African plan, accepted what he could not change.

The future course of the war was set. The United States would work for the defeat of Hitler in Europe, with a cross-Channel landing as its principal means. First, however, Britain and the United States would fight together to drive the Germans from North Africa and to establish Allied control from the Atlantic coast of Africa to the Suez Canal.

Such help as could be given to the Soviet Union would continue to be sent, both by northern convoy and, increasingly, by the trans-Persia Caspian route—Persia (now Iran) having been occupied jointly by the Soviet Union and Britain.

At Stalin's request the Anglo-American bombing of German cities would be intensified. But the timing of the "Second Front" would be determined in London and Washington, not in Moscow. There would be no cross-Channel landing in 1942, nor until such time as Churchill, Roosevelt, and their military advisers judged it to be a feasible operation. For the remaining four and a half months of 1942, North Africa would be the focal point of Anglo-American efforts.

On 19 August 1942, as preparations began for the North African landings, a European operation was carried out. This was a small-scale, predominantly Canadian cross-Channel raid against the Channel port of Dieppe. Designed to secure technical and Intelligence gains for the Allies as well as to test the defenses of the port, the Dieppe raid was undertaken on the insistence of the Chief of Combined Operations, Vice Admiral Lord Louis Mountbatten. The British Air Ministry had rejected his call for a substantial force of British heavy bombers, insisting that they were needed for the ongoing strategic air offensive against Germany.

The Dieppe raid made clear the problems that the much larger assault would face, of having not only to hold a swathe of territory, but also to drive the German forces back to Paris, Brussels, and, in due course, the Rhine. A factor that assisted the defenders was the fortified bunkers of the Atlantic Wall. Above all, the Dieppe raid highlighted the difficulties of attacking a defended port.

The principal force taking part in the Dieppe raid were 4,963 Canadian and 1,075 British troops. Also taking part were fifty American rangers and two dozen Free French soldiers, including Lieutenant Francis Vourch of No. 10 Inter-Allied Commando, who sixteen months later was to go ashore in Normandy on a pre-D-Day clandestine mission.

The Dieppe landing, code-named Operation Jubilee, was intended to be brief. Allied casualties were high; just over a thousand of the raiding force were killed—907 of them Canadian—and a further two thousand taken prisoner, while all vehicles and equipment had to be left behind on the beach. "This is the first time," mocked Hitler, "that the British have had the courtesy to cross the sea to offer the enemy a complete sample of their weapons." Later, however, Hitler warned his commanders: "We must realize that we are not alone in learning a lesson from Dieppe. The British have also learned. We must reckon with a totally different mode of attack and a quite different place."

Hitler was right. The British were already evolving a quite different cross-Channel strategy. On the day after the Dieppe raid, Mountbatten told the British War Cabinet that the lessons learned from the Dieppe raid would be "invaluable" in planning for the future cross-Channel invasion. Many years later he was to say that the Dieppe raid "gave the Allies the priceless secret of victory."

Three lessons in particular were learned at Dieppe, each of which was to have a direct impact on the Normandy landings. The first was that a frontal assault on a fortified harbor must not be attempted. This was overcome by the creation of floating harbors that could be assembled off the beach. The second lesson was that the assault troops in any cross-Channel landing must be accompanied by armored vehicles capable of defeating pillboxes. To meet this need, special floating tanks were devised. The third lesson related to security.

No attempt had been made at Dieppe—either by General Montgomery, who first devised the plan, or by Admiral Mountbatten, who eventually carried it out—to coordinate with the Inter-Services Security Board (ISSB), the organization charged with security and secrecy essential for military, naval, and air operations. For all future such operations, the ISSB was brought in as a matter of course. It was regarded as imperative that there should be no leakage or even hint of where an operation would take place. To this end, security was perfected to a remarkable degree, and deception was made a central part of the security scheme.

3

Toward Overlord

O nce Roosevelt had made it clear, in March 1942, that there could be no cross-Channel offensive until the summer of 1944, the British Chiefs of Staff had no alternative but to make plans for the new date, working in tandem with their American colleagues. Churchill accepted the reality and began at once to consider how a major amphibious landing should be facilitated. On May 30 he studied a Combined Operations outline titled "Piers for Use on Beaches," about the floating piers that would be essential to unload supplies from the landing ships once they had crossed the Channel. Churchill noted on the outline, in a handwritten comment on the piers (in which he underlined the word "must"): "They must float up & down w the tide. The anchor problem must be mastered. The ships must have a side-flap cut in them and a draw-bridge large enough to overreach the moorings of the piers. Let me have the best solution worked out. Don't argue the matter. The difficulties will argue for themselves."

Not only floating piers, but also complete artificial harbors, were designed to avoid dependence on the strongly fortified Channel ports: Cherbourg, Le Havre, Dieppe, and

Calais. Two concrete harbors were designed in such a way that they could be assembled in Britain, towed across the English Channel, and put in place off the French coast. An underwater pipeline was also being devised to enable fuel oil to be brought ashore once the landings had secured a base for the advance inland. It was known as PLUTO—Pipe Line Under the Ocean.

Not only plans, but also action, were under way. On the night of 3–4 September 1942, in the Channel Islands, twelve British commandos landed on a German lighthouse, which was also being used as a radio station. All seven Germans manning the lighthouse were captured together with their codebooks. Their radio equipment was destroyed. Four weeks later, in a conference with his senior advisers, Hitler mocked his advisers' assertion that the Atlantic Wall could not be broken. "Above all," he said, "I am grateful to the English for proving me right by their various landing attempts. It shows up those who think I am always seeing phantoms, who say, 'Well, when are the English coming? There is absolutely nothing happening on the coast—we swim every day, and we haven't seen a single Englishman!'"

Despite his mockery, Hitler accelerated the construction of the Atlantic Wall, which had already proved effective at Dieppe. That September, after a conference with his Armaments Minister, Albert Speer, and Field Marshal Gerd von Rundstedt, the building of the wall was placed under the Todt Organization, which, since the death of its head, Fritz Todt, seven months earlier, had been headed by Speer. Two million slave laborers were employed in the construction of the wall. Its planned 15,000 fortified strong points—concrete bunkers and gun batteries—were to be manned by 300,000 troops.

Allied and German preparations were going ahead in tandem. On November 5 a new British airborne unit, the 3rd Parachute Brigade, was formed. Of its 644 members, 567 were volunteers. Later it was to become part of a newly created 6th Airborne Division, which included a gliderborne brigade. The division's motto was "Go To It!" Training was rigorous, morale high, and the task ahead—to be the spearhead of any British amphibious landing in northern Europe—was daunting but accepted.

In November 1942 the Allied forces, predominantly American, landed in North Africa. The whole Mediterranean coastline of North Africa, from Egypt to Morocco, was in Allied hands. On the Eastern Front, the Soviets were battling to prevent the Germans from capturing Stalingrad and reaching the River Volga. Churchill, fearful, as he had been in the autumn of 1941, of a Soviet defeat—followed by the switching of millions of German troops from Russia to a massive amphibious assault on Britain—responded to Stalin's renewed appeals for a Second Front by pressing his advisers to agree to August or September 1943 as the date of the cross-Channel landing. But at a Staff Conference on 16 December 1942 the three Chiefs of Staff, headed by General Sir Alan Brooke, told him that the rate and scale of the American troop build-up in Britain was inadequate for the task.

Admiral Lord Louis Mountbatten, who had just returned from the United States and who was shortly to be appointed head of Combined Operations, informed Churchill and the Chiefs of Staff that, despite an agreement to the contrary, "the Americans were putting the good engines into their own landing craft and fitting ours with the unsatisfactory type." In addition, Mountbatten reported, many of the landing craft needed to transport a cross-Channel force were being diverted by the Americans to the war in the Pacific. Any hopes for a 1943 cross-Channel landing had been frustrated.

The need to reach agreement on the date of the cross-Channel landing called for a further meeting between Roosevelt and Churchill and their senior advisers. The meeting was held in Casablanca, starting on 13 January 1943. There, the British and American Combined Chiefs of Staff warned of the many problems of supply and preparation, with the result that agreement was reached not to launch the cross-Channel liberation of German-occupied Europe until the early summer of 1944. During the course of 1943 there would be an Anglo-American amphibious landing in the Mediterranean—against Sicily.

The results of the eight days of discussions at Casablanca were, Churchill reported to his War Cabinet, "from one point of view, very remarkable." The priority of "Hitler's extinction" as against Japan had been reestablished. Although priority had been secured for the Mediterranean over the cross-Channel assault that summer, it was not to interfere with the "maximum" development of the build-up in Britain of the forces that would be needed for a cross-Channel invasion in 1944. Slowly but inexorably, the scale and date of the Normandy landings were being determined. In their final report, presented to Churchill and Roosevelt, the Combined Chiefs of Staff proposed the build-up in Britain of fifteen divisions of trained and equipped American troops, amounting to 384,000 men by 15 August 1943, and 938,000 men by 31 December 1943. This would allow for five months of intensive training and enable the preparation of a limited raid—not the cross-Channel assault—to be launched from Britain against the northern coast of France during 1943. The "primary object" of this raid, in the words of the Combined Chiefs, was "of provoking air battles and causing enemy losses."

As well as this limited raid—which in the event never took place, being subsumed in the cross-Channel invasion—the Combined Chiefs of Staff also proposed preparing a second limited operation, to be launched against the Cotentin Peninsula, of which Cherbourg was the principal port. Set for 1 August 1943, it was aimed at "seizing and holding a bridgehead and, if the state of German morale and resources permit, at vigorously exploiting successes." This, too, never took place, being subsumed, like the fifteen division raid, into the cross-Channel invasion: the full-scale assault on German-ruled northern Europe.

Another decision made at Casablanca consisted of a round-the-clock Anglo-American bomber offensive, Operation Pointblank—the twenty-four-hour bombing of Germany: by day by American bombers based in Britain, and by night by British bombers long experienced in night attacks, as a prerequisite to a cross-Channel landing. The aim of Pointblank, which was to begin in May, and was to be carried out with an intensity hitherto unknown in aerial warfare, was, in the words of Roosevelt and Churchill's secret directive, to achieve not only "the progressive destruction and dislocation of the German military, industrial, and economic system," but also "the undermining of the morale of the German people to a point where their capacity for armed resistance is fatally weakened."

For the Soviets, despite the damage that would be wreaked on Germany's cities by the bombing, the Casablanca conclusions were grave disappointments. "Nothing in the world," Churchill noted later that day, "will be accepted by Stalin as an alternative to our placing fifty or sixty Divisions in France by the spring of this year. I think he will be disappointed and furious with the joint message. Therefore I thought it wise that the President and I should both stand together. After all, our backs are broad."

Following Casablanca, an Anglo-American planning staff was set up to prepare for the cross-Channel landings, which were given the code name Overlord. It was headed by Lieutenant General Sir Frederick Morgan, who had been among the troops evacuated from Dunkirk in 1940. No Supreme Allied Commander was to be appointed for almost a year. Morgan was made Chief of Staff, Supreme Allied Command. The acronym of his title, COSSAC, also became the name by which his organization was known.

Morgan and his COSSAC team were given two specific and intertwining tasks. The first was to plan for the cross-Channel landings. The second was to convince the Germans that the main Allied landing would be at the narrowest part of the Channel, facing the Pas-de-Calais. To achieve this, a deception plan was evolved, which was given the code name Bodyguard, Churchill having written that "In wartime, truth is so precious that she should always be attended by a bodyguard of lies." Without deception as to where the Allies would land, the Germans would be able to confront any landing attempt with their maximum forces.

To prepare the deception plan, General Morgan established a special section on his planning staff, which was given the innocuous name "Ops B." One main area of deception would depend on controlled leakage (known as "Special Means"). In charge of this was Roger Hesketh, a country house owner and amateur architect in civilian life.

He worked closely with Colonel John Bevan, the head of the London Controlling Section, responsible for the German agents who had been "turned" and were working for Britain. Bevan coordinated the work of those agents, ensuring that they played a central part in persuading the Germans that black was white—or, in geographic terms, that Normandy was the Pas-de-Calais.

The number of organizations involved in preparing for the cross-Channel assault was formidable, as was the number of personnel involved. The factories that produced the tanks, guns, planes, and ships worked twenty-four hours a day. Commando units were practicing throughout Britain (see the map on page 182). Specialist weapons were being devised and produced. Special units were being created. On May 6 the 6th Airborne Division was established, under Major General Richard Gale. It was to spearhead the assault on the eastern flank of the landings.

Security was an essential feature of the invasion plans. Starting in the spring of 1943 and gradually becoming more extensive, a "holiday ban" was imposed on people wishing to visit the North Sea, English Channel, and Bristol Channel coasts. This ban was seen as essential, not only to mask the real preparations but also to safeguard the deception "preparations." In addition, the Committee on Overlord Preparations was set up, chaired by Churchill, "to speed up and stimulate Overlord preparations in all aspects other than tactical and strategic, and to review and adjust their impact on war programs and the life of the community."

German power at sea was a formidable obstacle to any cross-Channel plans. German submarine dominance of the

Atlantic made the transit of American and Canadian troops a prospect of great danger. In the early summer of 1943 that danger began to wane. Indeed, a collapse of the U-boat successes was taking place, arising to a considerable extent out of a triumph of cryptography: the reading of the modified form of Enigma signals that were used by the U-boats in the Atlantic. By a remarkable cryptographic success, this modified Enigma had been broken in December 1942, and by the end of June 1943 the sinkings dropped below the danger level (sixty merchant ships had been sunk in March, thirty-four in April, thirty-one in May, and eleven in June). This had important repercussions in releasing warships and merchant ships for service in all theaters of war, including Operation Priceless, as the post-Sicily move against the Italian mainland was then known.

On May 14, in Washington, the British and American Chiefs of Staff, meeting as a single body, confirmed the priority for Operation Pointblank, the combined Anglo-American bomber offensive from air bases in Britain, with the ultimate aim "to permit initiation of final combined operations on the Continent"—operations for which almost one million American soldiers would be undergoing five months of intensive training in the United Kingdom.

Returning to the United States in May 1943, Churchill sought, in public, to stress both the strength of the Germans and the danger of not taking decisive action against them. Speaking to a joint session of Congress on May 19, he warned, "The enemy is still proud and powerful. He is hard to get at. He still possesses enormous armies, vast resources, and invaluable strategic territories." There was, Churchill said, "one grave danger," the "undue" prolongation of the war, and he went on to explain: "No one can tell what new complications and perils might arise in four or five more years of war. And it is in the dragging out of the war at enormous expense, until the democracies are tired or bored or split, that the main hopes of Germany and Japan must now reside."

Meeting in Washington that day, Churchill and Roosevelt determined that the cross-Channel landings would take place no later than 1 May 1944, whatever problems or opportunities might be created by the imminent invasion of Italy. They also agreed that the cross-Channel landings were to be carried out by twenty-nine divisions, with the possibility of a Free French division being added; in all, almost a million men.

The question of where the landings should take place was yet to be decided. In June a conference—code-named Rattle—was held between General Morgan and Admiral Mountbatten, and their staffs, at which it was agreed to make the assault on the Normandy beaches. It was also agreed to go ahead with the plan to build two vast floating harbors and take them across the Channel for use off the beaches. Within a month of the choice of Normandy, the Canadian 3rd Division was selected as part of the invasion force. It began training at once, in Scotland, and then in cooperation with the Royal Navy, at Portsmouth, England. It would have a landing area of its own.

Once Normandy had been decided on, another top-secret enterprise was created to enable it to succeed. This was Exercise PINWE—an acronym for "Problems of the Invasion of North-West Europe" (even the acronym could not be allowed to contain any clue as to the actual destination— a far cry from Lord Kitchener's "Constantinople Expeditionary Force" at the beginning of 1915). The task allotted to PINWE was to prepare detailed maps of the Normandy area, marking on them every feature and obstacle.

Among those working on these essential maps was Harold Pickersgill—a man remembered to this day in Normandy, where he landed with his Reconnaisance Corps regiment, married, and made his home after the war. There he discovered, only after some twenty years, that his own physician, Dr. Sustendal, had been one of the main French informants for the PINWE team—for which he had been awarded the Légion d'Honneur.

An integral component of the cross-Channel preparations was the participation of the French Resistance in acts of sabotage. To sustain and enhance this, SOE had established numerous circuits inside France, with British agents giving instructions and help. These agents, and their circuits, were in constant danger. The head of the Prosper circuit, Major Francis Suttill, supervised the work of nearly thirty British-trained agents. For nine months he had helped set up and arm Resistance networks around Paris. On June 24, as a result of a German security service success, he, his wireless operator, and his courier/lieutenant were arrested by the Gestapo, followed over the next two to three months by the arrest of a thousand Resistance workers associated with his efforts. Four hundred were killed, including Suttill, who was tortured after his arrest and died in the Sachsenhausen concentration camp in March 1945. The Germans saw the breakup of Prosper as a triumph. Hitler himself "believed, or at any rate hoped"—in the words of the SOE historian Professor M. R. D. Foot—"that the breakup of Suttill's circuit represented a serious setback for the Anglo-American plans to liberate France."

Comparing the work of Suttill and his Prosper network

with that of a group of sappers during the Normandy landings (the "Neptune" coast), M. R. D. Foot writes: "Before
the main invading forces could actually set foot, a little after
sunrise, on the Neptune coast, three battalions of British
sappers had to go ashore at low tide with the first light of
early dawn, and make safe the mine-laden obstacles strewn
on the beaches. Three-quarters of them were shot down at
their work; but they did it. Suttill and his colleagues were
doing a similar indispensable pioneers' task; their fate was no
more agreeable for being so much more protracted, yet
their relatives also can feel they died to some good purpose."
The death of Suttill and the destruction of so much effort
and achievement did not halt the work of establishing agents
in France, of coordinating the activities of the French Resistance, or of gaining information that would help the eventual
landings. As well as the Resistance, British and French commandos in Britain were enlisted to help collect information
about the landing beaches. Between July and December
1943 they carried out six raids across the Channel. Their task
was twofold: their own visual "field" Intelligence-gathering,
including samples of barbed wire from the beach, and the
information provided by German soldiers whom they captured and brought back to Britain as prisoners of war. British
and French commandos worked side by side. The French
commando troop was headed by Captain Philippe Kieffer,
who was to take part in the Normandy landings.

The Allied armies, waiting for their new task in the early
summer of 1944, were not to be idle in the remaining six
months of 1943. Indeed, an ambitious plan, for the invasion
of Italy, put forward by the Combined Chiefs of Staff, was
approved by Roosevelt and Churchill. A convoy of Ameri-

can troops on their way to Britain had been diverted by the Americans to the Mediterranean, for Eisenhower's use in the Italian campaign.

The demands and opportunities of the Italian campaign led Churchill—six months after Casablanca and despite Casablanca's considerable plans for the cross-Channel landings—to question the very basis of the cross-Channel decision. Advancing northward through Italy could prove an active, successful Second Front instead, forcing Hitler to divert forces from the Eastern Front.

Churchill's view was made known to General Wedemeyer when he visited London on July 26 for a conference with the COSSAC planners; the Chief of the Imperial General Staff, General Sir Alan Brooke; and Churchill's Chief of Staff, General Sir Hastings Ismay. In his report to Washington, Wedemeyer urged the appointment of a Supreme Commander designate for the cross-Channel landings (Operation Overlord), with his own staff. Wedemeyer favored Sir Charles Portal, Chief of the Air Staff, as Supreme Commander, believing that of all the candidates Portal was the most impressive; but Portal was British, and, as Wedemeyer explained to his superiors in Washington, the United States "will have a preponderance of forces, both surface and air, as the Overlord operation unfolds."

Wedemeyer then reported on Churchill's attitude to Overlord, not disguising the rift that had opened between the planners and the Prime Minister. Churchill, he wrote, ". . . Is seeking every honorable avenue by which to escape British commitment to such an operation. Some of the British planners are enthusiastically supporting Overlord; others are paying lip service to that concept but are advocating continuing operations in the Mediterranean; and there are others who would welcome operations in the Balkans."

In addition, Wedemeyer reported, Churchill "has recalled the Norway operation for examination, and I would not be surprised if such an operation were not strongly presented by the British at Quadrant." The Quadrant Conference was to be convened in Quebec, to sort out the conflicting plans that had begun to emerge, despite the firm decision at Casablanca on the cross-Channel landings. Although the British planners were examining the Overlord plan that had recently been completed by General Morgan's staff, Wedemeyer warned Washington that "the recent diversion of the convoy to Eisenhower's theater, thus reducing troop movements to the UK, has been seized upon by the opponents of Overlord as an excuse for a complete reexamination of that operation. . . ."

Churchill knew that at a certain point late in 1943 or early in 1944, under the COSSAC plan, seven divisions in the Mediterranean Theater would be withdrawn for participation in the cross-Channel invasion. He also knew that if the Italian campaign were to prosper, its continuing success might become impossible if those divisions were taken away. Yet even with the transfer of these seven divisions, Churchill wrote to the Chiefs of Staff Committee on July 19 that it might be felt that the forces available in the United Kingdom "will not be equal to the task of landing and maintaining themselves on land." If so, Churchill wanted the northern Norway landing, Operation Jupiter, to be considered instead of Overlord for the spring of 1944. "In my view it is a preferable alternative," he wrote, "and, in all probability, the only one which will be open in the west."

Churchill then set out what he had come to believe was the "right strategy" for 1944. It was in two parts, and would include both the Italian front and the northern Norway expedition, with the cross-Channel invasion taking a different role. The first of the strategies set out by Churchill was the "maximum" advance through Italy once Sicily was secured. This advance should be continued—"certainly"—as far as the River Po, "with an option to attack westwards in the south of France or north-eastwards towards Vienna." At the same time, the Allies should seek "to procure the expulsion of the enemy from the Balkans and Greece." The second part of this strategy for 1944 was the northern Norway expedition, with Overlord used as a cover. Churchill then explained why he felt that Jupiter should replace Overlord:

"I do not believe that twenty-seven Anglo-American divisions are sufficient for Overlord in view of the extraordinary fighting efficiency of the German army, and the much larger forces they could so readily bring to bear against our troops even if the landings were successfully accomplished. It is right for many reasons to make every preparation with the utmost sincerity and vigour, but if later on it is realised by all concerned that the operation is beyond our strength in May and will have to be postponed till August 1944, then it is essential that we should have this other considerable operation up our sleeves." Churchill added: "We cannot allow our Metropolitan forces to remain inert."

For the Allies, the military developments on the battlefields were auspicious omens. "The massed, angered forces of common humanity," Roosevelt told the American people during his Fireside Chat broadcast on July 28, "are on the march. They are going forward—on the Russian front, in the vast Pacific area, and into Europe—converging upon their ultimate objectives, Berlin and Tokyo." His words "into Europe" referred to Italy. There, Roosevelt declared, "The first crack in the Axis has come. The criminal, corrupt Fascist regime in Italy is going to pieces."

Churchill's preference for Norway rather than Normandy was a serious one. If the cross-Channel strategy—and date— were to be finalized, and the Casablanca decisions made good, it would have to be decided at Quebec. On the afternoon of 5 August 1943, Churchill and the three British Chiefs of Staff sailed on the *Queen Mary* from the River Clyde. They used the five-day trans-Atlantic voyage to discuss every aspect of the war plans for the year ahead, predominant among them the cross-Channel invasion, on which so much preparatory work had been done in the previous six months.

The trans-Atlantic crossing was Churchill's first opportunity to learn from his advisers the full details of the Overlord plan, including the progress made toward creating two artificial harbors that were to be assembled in England, taken across the Channel, and then used to enable the Allied forces to get ashore and to be supplied across what had hitherto been open beaches.

The plan for the artificial harbors was presented to Churchill by Brigadier K. G. McLean, who, with two other officers from General Morgan's COSSAC staff, had been working since the Casablanca Conference to devise a workable plan to land on the Normandy beaches. The main proposal was to use airborne troops to secure a landing zone; COSSAC had in mind at that time a direct airborne assault on the town of Caen, eight miles inland.

Churchill later recalled how Brigadier McLean and the

two other officers "came to me as I lay in my bed in the spacious cabin, and, after they had set up a large-scale map, explained in a tense and cogent tale the plan which had been prepared for the cross-Channel descent upon France."

Brigadier McLean then explained that the artificial harbors, code-named Mulberry, would be created by block ships, code-named Gooseberries—old naval and merchant vessels that would cross the Channel under their own power and then be sunk in prearranged positions, to form a continuous breakwater within which supply ships could dock and unload.

The head of Churchill's defense staff, General Ismay, later recalled how, "If a stranger had visited his bathroom, he might have seen a stocky figure in a dressing-gown of many colours, sitting on a stool and surrounded by a number of what our American friends call 'Top Brass,' while an Admiral flapped his hand in the water at one end of the bath in order to simulate a choppy sea, and a Brigadier stretched a lilo across the middle to show how it broke up the waves. The stranger would have found it hard to believe that this was the British High Command studying the most stupendous and spectacular amphibious operation in the history of war."

On the afternoon of 19 August 1943, at Quebec, the Combined Chiefs of Staff presented Roosevelt and Churchill with their conclusions, which the two leaders accepted. Germany was to be defeated before Japan; this was the "overall strategic concept." The cross-Channel landings, Operation Overlord, were to constitute the "primary United States-British ground and air effort against the Axis in Europe," with the assault set for 1 May 1944. The aim of Overlord was not only a landing in northern France, but also the undertaking of further operations from northern France "designed to strike at the heart of Germany and to destroy her military forces."

It was also decided at Quebec that the Allied invasion of Italy would take place before the end of the month, with Naples as its objective. In the Balkans, Allied activity would be "limited" to sending supplies by air and sea to the guerrillas, to the use of "minor Commando forces," and to the bombing of strategic objectives.

The Combined Chiefs of Staff were also agreed, and Churchill and Roosevelt accepted, that as between Overlord and operations in the Mediterranean, wherever there was a shortage of resources, "available resources will be distributed and employed with the main object of ensuring the success of Overlord." Only if circumstances were to render Overlord impossible would the Allies consider the northern Norway landing, Operation Jupiter, as an alternative, expanded to include "an entry into southern Norway."

In Italy, "unremitting pressure" was to be maintained against the German forces and the creation of what the Combined Chiefs of Staff described as "conditions required for Overlord." The Combined Chiefs of Staff also proposed, in order to create "a diversion in connection with Overlord, an Allied lodgement" in southern France, in the Toulon-Marseille area, with exploitation northward.

During his discussions with Roosevelt on August 19 about the Combined Chiefs of Staff report, Churchill expressed his worry lest Overlord were to be carried out against too formidable a German military defense. To guard against this he sought, and obtained, the President's agreement to the rule proposed by General Morgan and his

COSSAC team, whereby if there were more than twelve mobile German divisions in France at the intended moment of the Allied landing, that landing would not take place. Nor, as Morgan had advised, should the Germans be capable of a build-up of more than fifteen divisions "in the succeeding two months."*

Churchill's primary fear was casualties. "We had the most solemn warnings of what might happen," Roosevelt's confidant Harry Hopkins told Churchill's doctor on August 20. "The old, old story of enormous casualties and the terrific strength of the German fortifications." But having given his warnings, Churchill accepted that Overlord should go ahead. He "wished to emphasize," as the minutes of the meeting recorded, "that he strongly favored Overlord for 1944," and he asked that every effort be made "to add at least 25 percent to the initial assault." There were nine months, he pointed out, in which to ensure an increase in the number of landing craft available. The beaches selected were "good," he told the meeting, "but it would be better if at the same time a landing were to be made on the inside beaches of the Cotentin Peninsula." Churchill added: "The initial lodgement must be strong, as it largely affects later operations."

On 3 September 1943, the fourth anniversary of Britain's declaration of war on Germany, the Western Allies launched Operation Baytown, the invasion of mainland Italy. At

---

*On 6 June 1944 (D-Day), the fighting power of the German military divisions in France did not exceed General Morgan's limits. The build-up of German divisions in the succeeding two months did not significantly exceed those limits in fighting power.

four-thirty that morning, formations of the British Eighth Army, commanded by General Montgomery, crossed the Strait of Messina to land at Reggio di Calabria.

As British and Canadian troops came ashore, the Italian government adhered to the terms of the armistice conditions that no Italian troops would go into action against the invading forces. The armistice itself was signed in Sicily that afternoon, to come into public and formal effect in five days. It was the German army that would have to defend what was, in effect, a second front on the continent of Europe. Unknown to them, as they hurried reinforcements into southern Italy, the cross-Channel landings were a mere nine months away.

Above France, the night of September 12 was the night of Operation Battering Ram, when, as part of the SOE work with the French Resistance, three British pilots flew eight members of the Resistance to a rendezvous in the center of France, and they took off with eight more back to Britain. Those brought to France included Colonel Marchal, who was arrested ten days later and who avoided interrogation by taking his cyanide pill. Another of the passengers, Colonel Jarry, was later arrested, tortured, and shot.

4

Preparations
Intensify

Even as the Allied invasion of Italy became the main Allied focus, the cross-Channel landings were never out of the minds of those at the center of war policy. After studying the daily telegraphic reports from the British Commander-in-Chief, Mediterranean, General Sir Harold Alexander, Churchill felt "easier," he informed Roosevelt on September 18, about the Salerno landings on the Italian mainland, but he went on to warn Roosevelt that "the quality of German resistance shows how hard we shall have to fight in Overlord."

Responsibility for the design and production of the two Mulberry harbors needed for Overlord was given to the Directorate of Ports and Inland Water Transport, headed by Sir Bruce White. Under him a special staff, known as X Staff, was installed in Norfolk House, St. James's Square, London, under Commodore Cecil Hughes-Hallett, Director of Plans at the Admiralty. Also being prepared by the X Staff were sixty ships, most of them merchantmen but also an old battleship and three cruisers, that were to be towed across the Channel, without engines or guns, but filled with concrete, to create on D-Day artificial break-waters known as "Gooseberries," to provide protection for landing craft and supply ships.

On the South Coast of Britain the first training courses were held that September at the Assault Training Center, at Saunton Sands. The center was commanded by an American officer, Lieutenant Colonel Paul W. Thompson, one of the many men who were to play a major part in the intricate work of preparation. All the American troops destined to land on Utah and Omaha Beaches trained there, except for those who had already been tested in the fighting in North Africa and Sicily.

To load the tanks, armored vehicles, and trucks onto the landing craft, outlets from more than fifty beaches in Britain were chosen and had to be made ready. This was done by constructing hardened ramps, known as "hards," which could only be built when the tide was out. These hards were needed not only for the embarkations themselves but also for the training embarkations that were repeated until they were as flawless as possible. Many of them can still be seen on the South Coast today. At one of them, first used to load supplies for the Channel crossing on D-Day, the first German prisoners of war were to be disembarked the following night.

Another area of preparation was being supervised by Major General Sir Percy Hobart, Montgomery's brother-in-law and a leading expert on tank warfare. Churchill had known Hobart since he had been given command of the very first tank brigade, set up in 1934. Since 1940 Hobart, having been out of favor with the War Office, was serving as a corporal in the Home Guard. At Churchill's urging he was recalled in 1943 to command the 79th Armoured Division, with a single aim: to develop armor that could accompany a seaborne assault.

The specialized armored vehicles devised and produced under Hobart's keen eye were given the title Armoured Vehicle Royal Engineers (AVRE). They were also known as "Hobart's Funnies." Seven of his designs were to see action in Normandy. One was the floating tank, the DD "Duplex Drive," known colloquially as "Donald Duck." Its engine power could be transferred from its tracks to twin propellers and, by erecting a high canvas screen around it, the "tank" could float. Once onshore, power was returned to the tracks and the screen jettisoned. So secret were the amphibious tanks that their sea training, in the Solent, could take place only at night. Sometimes the training took place in the middle of shipping lanes. As one observer noted: "Ship's officers could not believe their eyes when they switched on a spotlight and saw this strange collection of canvas boats roaming aimlessly, and received a greeting of real Canadian curses."

Then there were the Crocodiles—tanks modified to be flamethrowers. These were followed by Crabs: tanks fitted with an extended pair of arms carrying a flail. Their purpose was to clear minefields by beating the mines to force them to explode. They could do their work of minesweeping at one and a half miles per hour.

Another of Hobart's Funnies was the Beach Armoured Recovery Vehicle (BARV), a tank whose gun turret was replaced by a superstructure that allowed the tank to drive into deep water and, through fitted winches or small dozer blades, to clear beaches of stranded vehicles. Bobbin was a tank adapted to carry a 110-yard-long spool of flexible coir coconut matting that could be laid in front of the vehicle to form a road over soft or slippery ground for itself and following vehicles. The Armoured Ramp Carrier (ARK) was a turretless tank carrying two runways across its flat top. It could be used to provide a ramped road up and over a beach wall, or it could be dropped into ditches or streams to form a bridge.

Other Hobart's Funnies included armored vehicles carrying enormous two-ton bundles of wood called fascines—first experimented with in the First World War—that were used to fill holes in roadways, bridge layers, and craned recovery vehicles. Known as Petard, this vehicle was based on a tank chassis, with its normal main armament replaced by a short-barreled mortar that fired a "flying dustbin" explosive charge. Its function was to destroy enemy pillboxes and fixed obstructions.

The Americans also had an amphibious landing vehicle, the DUKW (the "duck"). A six-wheeled truck, boat-shaped, it got its name from its factory serial number initials: D = the year of the model, U = amphibian, K = all-wheel drive, and W = dual rear axles.

Preparations, devices, and plans were taking place throughout Britain at an ever-increasing tempo. The 6th Airborne Division, which had been established in May, was also making plans. It was commanded by Major General Richard Gale, whose airborne soldiers would have to capture two strategic bridges over the River Orne, between the sea and Caen. In May 1940 the Germans had struck one of their first blows against the Belgians by seizing the fort of Eben Emael by paratroop assault. Gale had studied that dramatic descent and decided to emulate it. Training was to begin in the New Year.

In German-occupied France, the Resistance and SOE

were extending their areas of operation. In September 1943, Michel Pichard (code name Oyster), who had joined De Gaulle's Free French forces two years earlier, was given responsibility throughout the northern half of France for coordination of Royal Air Force drops to help the Resistance. At the age of twenty-five, he supervised the work of five hundred dropping zones.

The landing of agents into France was undertaken by 161 Squadron, Royal Air Force, led by Hugh Verity. During 1943 he himself flew twenty-nine missions, landing his single-engined Lysander by moonlight, as did all his pilots, in fields marked by the French Resistance with fires or flares. A single Morse identifying letter, flashed and returned, would be the sole contact between the pilot and those awaiting him on the ground. The average time that each Lysander was on the ground, dropping agents off and picking agents up for the return journey, was a mere three minutes.

Hitler was also advancing his defensive preparations against any invasion attempt. That same September, construction began of the massive fortified gun battery at le Chaos, on the Normandy coast five miles inland from Bayeux—a British objective on the first day of the Normandy landings. The battery comprised four gun positions, a two-storied observation bunker, anti-aircraft guns, defense works, and searchlights.

On October 28, Field Marshal Gerd von Rundstedt, Commander-in-Chief, West, gave Hitler an assessment on what he believed to be the three most likely points of an Allied invasion. These were the Channel coast, the French Riviera, and the Bay of Biscay, possibly in some combination. Sent by top-secret radio signal, von Rundstedt's assessment was decrypted by the codebreakers at Bletchley Park, north of

London, and sent to Churchill and the Chiefs of Staff, as well as to the Americans.

Hitler was also focusing his attention on where an Allied invasion might come. He sensed a strong likelihood of a cross-Channel attack, which he thought would come in the spring of 1944, or possibly even earlier. On November 3 he issued Führer Directive No. 51, setting out his plans to counter the invasion. The danger in the East remained, he wrote, "but a greater danger now appears in the West: an Anglo-Saxon landing!" In the East, because of the vastness of the territory involved, large areas could be lost "without a fatal blow being dealt to the nervous system of Germany," but in the West, he warned, "Should the enemy succeed in breaching our defenses here on a wide front, the immediate consequences would be unpredictable."

Hitler was about to face an adversary he was never to see or know about. On November 20 the Chiefs of Staff were presented with a plan to deceive him totally as to where the Allied landings would take place. The authors of the plan were the London Controlling Section, headed by Colonel John Bevan, and the Ops B arm of General Morgan's staff. The historian of strategic deception, Sir Michael Howard, has described the plan as "perhaps the most complex and successful operation in the entire history of war." At first it did not even have a code name, but was referred to as "Appendix Y." The implementation of its directive during the coming seven months was to ensure the success of the Normandy landings.

The directive was succinct and bold, its three short paragraphs outlining one of the most remarkable examples of wartime deception. First, "To induce the German Command to believe that the main assault and follow-up will be in or east of the Pas-de-Calais area, thereby encouraging the enemy to maintain or increase the strength of his air and ground forces and his fortifications there at the expense of other areas, particularly of the Caen area." Second, "To keep the enemy in doubt as to the date and time of the actual assault." Third, "During and after the main assault, to contain the largest possible German land and air forces in or east of the Pas-de-Calais for at least fourteen days."

All was set to move forward with the wider strategic implications of the cross-Channel landing. Meeting in Cairo on November 23, Churchill, Roosevelt, and their staffs were told by General Eisenhower, then Allied Commander-in-Chief, Mediterranean, that he wanted the Italian campaign to be the main thrust of Allied strategy. In support of this priority, Eisenhower emphasized "the vital importance of continuing the maximum possible operations in an established theater since much time was invariably lost when the scene of action was changed, necessitating as it did the arduous task of building up a fresh base."

But the Italian campaign, with its prospect both of drawing large German forces deep into Italy, and of destroying them, would have to be subordinated to the cross-Channel plans. This was made clear two days later, when Churchill and Roosevelt, having flown eastward from Cairo to the Persian capital, Teheran, joined with Stalin in the first Big Three conference of the war. Stalin was traveling outside the Soviet Union for the first time since the Bolshevik Revolution of 1917.

Stalin stressed at Teheran that the forces of the Soviet Union—of which he was Generalissimo—were depending on the start of the Second Front in northern Europe in

1944. Churchill then told Stalin of the conditions, decided three months earlier, on which the launching of a cross-Channel assault depended. First, that there must be a "satisfactory reduction" in the strength of the German fighter forces in northwestern Europe before the assault. Second, the German reserves in France and the Low Countries must not on the day of the assault be more than "about twelve full-strength first-quality mobile divisions." Third, it must not be possible for the Germans to transfer from other fronts more than fifteen first-quality mobile divisions during the first sixty days of the operation.

In response to this, Stalin asked Churchill if "the Prime Minister and the British Staffs really believe in Overlord." Churchill replied that provided those conditions were met, "it will be our stern duty to hurl across the Channel against the Germans every sinew of our strength." Churchill and Roosevelt assured Stalin that the cross-Channel assault would take place "some time in May." Stalin then pressed Churchill and Roosevelt to tell him who would command the cross-Channel landing. Roosevelt said he would do so within a few days.

Eisenhower was the man chosen. In the conduct of the war in Tunisia, Sicily, and mainland Italy he had shown great skill in maintaining a strong, unified Allied command structure and in working effectively with the British officers serving under him. Returning to Cairo, Roosevelt informed Eisenhower of his choice on December 7. There was to be no turning back from the Overlord enterprise, complex and fraught with danger though it was. By the beginning of December the United States 9th Infantry Division had moved from Sicily—where it had been in action until August—to Britain. Its battle experience had begun a year earlier, with the Torch amphibious landings in North Africa. In Britain it was to continue training for the next six months. The expansion of amphibious landing practice was continuous. On December 1 nine hundred villagers were evacuated from the area of Tarbat Ness in Scotland, to make way for large-scale British landing exercises.

British and American planners had also begun their search—by means of aerial photoreconnaissance—for fields near potential landing beaches that could be turned into airfields within days of being overrun. Those beaches were already under another sort of scrutiny. On December 12 Hitler appointed Field Marshal Erwin Rommel to command the Atlantic Wall defenses. His task was to ensure that the coastline was properly fortified against any attempted Allied landing, wherever it might come. Rommel—the Desert Fox—had been the scourge of the British forces in North Africa until defeated at El Alamein and pushed back to Tunis by Montgomery's Eighth Army. Rommel's retreat, however, had been as impressive as his advance, with several victories on the way. Rommel's new responsibilities extended from Holland to the Atlantic coast of France.

On taking up his appointment, Rommel toured the coastline from Holland to the Cotentin Peninsula and was shocked at the gaps in and weaknesses of the Atlantic Wall. His immediate superior took the same view. "It all looks very black to me," von Rundstedt told him when they met in Paris shortly before Christmas. In a report to Hitler on the last day of the year, Rommel stressed that he thought the main Allied effort would be made "between Boulogne and the Somme estuary and on either side of Calais." Allied deception plans were to seek to confirm this misjudgment, and they succeeded in doing so.

Despite his focus on the wrong area, Rommel undertook to strengthen the whole coastline from the Cotentin Peninsula to Denmark. One of his first efforts was to organize a series of underwater obstacles that would trap and kill any invaders trying to wade ashore at high or even medium tide. One particularly fierce obstacle was a pattern of metal spikes clamped together, making the beach almost impassable. Many Allied soldiers were to perish as a result of it.

From Cairo, Roosevelt flew westward to Tunis, where, on December 7—the second anniversary of Pearl Harbor—he was met by Eisenhower, who as yet knew nothing of his appointment as Supreme Commander of the cross-Channel assault. As the two men drove together from the airport, Roosevelt turned to Eisenhower with the words "Well, Ike, you are going to command Overlord." Eisenhower replied, "Mr. President, I realize that such an appointment involved difficult decisions. I hope you will not be disappointed."

Eisenhower built up a strong team for his new task. Many had worked under him before. As his Deputy Supreme Commander he appointed a senior British airman, Air Chief Marshal Sir Arthur Tedder, who had served as Commander-in-Chief, Mediterranean Allied Air Forces, in the Tunisian and Italian campaigns. As Chief of Staff, he had a fellow American, his former Chief of Staff in the North African and Mediterranean campaigns, Lieutenant General Walter Bedell Smith.

To command the cross-Channel land forces—the 21st Army Group—was a British General, Sir Bernard Montgomery, a veteran of the Dunkirk evacuation. As commander of the Eighth Army, Montgomery had led the forces that defeated Rommel at El Alamein and had then driven him across North Africa to final defeat in Tunisia, after which Montgomery had commanded the Eighth Army in Sicily and Italy. Writing later about Montgomery, Eisenhower stressed that he had "no superior in two most important characteristics." The first was that "He quickly developed among British enlisted men an intense devotion and admiration—the greatest personal asset a commander can possess." The second characteristic was Montgomery's "tactical ability in what might be called the 'prepared' battle. In the study of enemy positions and situations and in the combining of his own armor, artillery, air, and infantry to secure tactical success against the enemy, he was careful, meticulous, and certain."

Another British Dunkirk veteran, Admiral Sir Bertram Ramsay, became Allied Naval Commander-in-Chief, Expeditionary Force (ANCXF). He had helped plan the North African Torch landing, which Eisenhower had commanded. An American soldier, Lieutenant General Omar N. Bradley, who had fought in Tunisia and Sicily—and whom Eisenhower called his "Eyes and Ears" in North Africa—was chosen to command the United States First Army.

"The war is now reaching the stage," Roosevelt warned the American people on Christmas Day 1943, "when we shall have to look forward to large casualty lists—dead, wounded, and missing." And he added, "War entails just that. There is no easy road to victory. And the end is not yet in sight."

The end was indeed not in sight, but certainly it was being systematically prepared for. On December 27, when

Churchill was in the Moroccan town of Marrakech, recuperating from illness, Eisenhower and Montgomery flew to see him. The two generals discussed their plans for the cross-Channel landing, explaining to Churchill how massive the assault would be. Four days later Churchill telegraphed to Stalin that everything was going "full blast" for Overlord and that Montgomery was "full of zeal to engage the enemy and of confidence in the result." As commander of the victorious Eighth Army in North Africa, Montgomery was a symbol of British determination.

As 1943 came to an end, a second set of Anglo-French commando operations was in preparation, code-named Hardtack. The men involved were part of No. 10 Inter-Allied Commando, known officially as No. 10 (IA) Commando. The first raid, Hardtack Dog, designed as a test, was carried out on the night of November 26–27 against Biville, east of Dieppe, which had earlier been the objective of an earlier raid. The first full raid, code-named Hardtack 11, was carried out on Christmas Eve by a French commando troop. Setting off from Dover by motor torpedo boat, the nine men got ashore by dinghy at Pointe de Gravelines, but there was an accident to the dinghy as they were returning to the boat. All nine were drowned.

On the night of December 26–27, Hardtack 21 was carried out by a French commando troop based in Britain. The raid was commanded by Lieutenant Francis Vourch, who had earlier taken part in the Dieppe raid. He and five French soldiers went ashore at Quinéville, on the Cotentin Peninsula, just north of what was to be the Allies' most westerly landing zone. Their objective was to locate and report on the antitank obstacles in the beach area. They found, and were able to describe in detail, an antitank obstacle known as Element C, constructed of steel girders and weighing some 2½ tons. This was to be one of the main beach defenses built under Rommel's direction.

The information Lieutenant Vourch and his five fellow commandos took back about Element C was to be of great value, helping the Allied planners to identify these obstacles and make efforts to destroy or bypass them. The French commandos also took back to Britain soil samples, in waterproof bags, to show the nature of the ground on which the soldiers and their armor would be landing.

The Quinéville raid was one of thirteen Hardtack raids to secure small but precious details to facilitate the landings. The bravery of those who made these raids was considerable. Like the members of the French Resistance who, both along the coast and inland, were also collecting similar evidence, they risked their lives, unseen and unsung.

5

Planning and Deception

On 2 January 1944, there was a dramatic Soviet advance on the Eastern Front. "Russians 27 miles from Poland," was the banner headline in the British *Sunday Express,* followed by a second line: "300 more towns taken in great surge towards frontier." The Allied planners were less exultant. They knew, through their clandestine reading of secret telegrams sent by neutral ambassadors, that Hitler's deliberate policy was to yield territory in the East in order to build up his forces and defenses in the West.

Although he did not know where an Allied invasion would land, Hitler knew that it must come. But he had faith in new weapons as yet untested in battle, including jet-propelled aircraft. "If I get the jets in time," he told two of his senior advisers on January 4, "I can fight off the invasion with them." Hitler had in mind more than a momentary respite in the use of jet aircraft. "If I get a few hundred of them to the front line," he remarked a few days later, "it will exorcise the specter of invasion for all time."

German propaganda broadcasts reflected concern about a possible cross-Channel invasion. On January 4, broadcasting from Berlin, the radio propagandist William Joyce—known derisively to his British listeners as Lord Haw-Haw, on account of his accent—asked: "Can the ordinary British soldier understand why he should have been expected to die in 1939 or 1940 or 1941 to restore an independent Poland on the old scale, whilst today he must die in order that the Soviets may rule Europe?"

This question hinted at a new situation on the ground. On January 6 Soviet forces crossed the 1939 Polish-Soviet border and advanced twelve miles inside it. Five days earlier, Stalin had established a Polish National Council to be the "supreme organ of democratic elements" in Poland. Predominantly Communist and under Moscow's control, it was to have its own armed forces and administration, in direct challenge to the Polish government in exile in London.

In Britain, as part of the training for the cross-Channel landings, Exercise Duck I was held on the South Coast on January 3 and 4 at Slapton Sands, the local inhabitants having been evacuated. Live ammunition was used from the shore as the American troops left their landing craft. On the first day of Duck I, General Montgomery, having given up command of the Eighth Army in Italy and flown to Britain, set up his headquarters—as Ground Force Commander of the Allied Expeditionary Forces—in his old school, St. Paul's School, in West London. On his first day at work he was given a presentation of the invasion plan drawn up by General Morgan and his COSSAC staff six months earlier.

Montgomery was critical of the narrow front assigned to the assaulting troops and succeeded in having that front extended, both westward, to include the beaches across the

Carentan estuary—later to become the Utah landing area—and eastward, to include the high ground and German gun batteries across the River Orne. The COSSAC plan envisaged an initial assault by three divisions. Montgomery increased that to five, with a two-division follow-up. That, he believed, was the "minimum . . . to make a proper success of the operation."

Part of the COSSAC plan that Montgomery studied on January 3 was a direct airborne assault on Caen by two-thirds of an airborne division. Montgomery rejected any such initial airborne assault seven miles and more inland from the beach areas. Instead, he proposed to use three airborne divisions to secure the beach landing areas: two American airborne divisions at the western end of an enlarged assault area and one British at the enlarged eastern end. Under Montgomery's plan, Caen would be the objective of the landing forces on the evening of the first day, advancing from the beaches that the airborne troops had secured during the early hours of the morning.

Montgomery's proposed changes to the COSSAC plan would have to be approved by the Supreme Commander, Allied Expeditionary Forces. But Eisenhower had not yet reached Britain, and for seven days, starting on January 14, Montgomery inspected and talked to the troops in training under his command: American, British, Canadian, Dutch, Czech, Belgian, and Polish, more than one million men in all.

On January 15, twelve days after Montgomery had been shown the COSSAC plan, and a day after he had begun his first tour of inspection of United States troops, the Supreme Commander, Allied Expeditionary Forces, General Eisenhower, who had just flown from the United States, took up his post in Britain. His headquarters were in Grosvenor Square, London—where, forty-five years later, he was to be honored, posthumously, by a statue.

Eisenhower's London office was in the headquarters of his old command, the European Theater of Operations, United States Army (ETOUSA). With his arrival it became Supreme Headquarters, Allied Expeditionary Forces, and acquired a new acronym, SHAEF. On January 21, six days after Eisenhower had reached London, he agreed, at his first full meeting with his commanders, to make the changes in the COSSAC plan that Montgomery had advised. The coastline on which the Allied troops would land extended for fifty miles. Long as that was, it was less than 10 percent of the 600-mile coastline from Denmark to Spain that the Germans were defending; and the Allied deception planners were determined to keep it that way.

Two other important decisions were made during that day-long meeting: the five divisions must land simultaneously, and port facilities must be provided on the Normandy shore, even if they had to be brought across the Channel.

The increase in the number of divisions over and above the original COSSAC plan would require a substantial increase in landing craft: an additional 47 large tank-carrying ships (LSTs, or Landing Ships, Tank, in military parlance), 144 tank landing craft (LCTs), 72 large infantry craft (LCI-Ls), 5 cruisers, and 24 destroyers. This extra burden was telegraphed to the Combined Chiefs of Staff in Washington on January 23. Eight days later the Combined Chiefs replied: Eisenhower's increases were all approved. Montgomery's enlarged plan could go ahead.

On January 15, the day on which Eisenhower entered his London headquarters, the first of sixty-eight landing ships were transferred from the Mediterranean Theater to Britain. To obtain the thousand extra landing craft required by Eisenhower, orders were given to build all the types of extra landing ships needed in the shipyards of the United States. This was done, achieving what General Marshall later called "a miracle of production." Thirteen American shipyards were enlisted to produce the necessary numbers on time, four of them on the inland waterways of the Ohio River. With shipyard workers doing a seventy-hour week, it proved possible to produce one ship every four and a half days, and, as the date for the cross-Channel D-Day drew closer, every three and a half days.

As a result of the priority given to the landing craft needed for Overlord, the Allied war effort against Japan had to suffer. At Cairo, Churchill and Roosevelt had promised the Chinese Nationalist leader, General Chiang Kai-shek, that in the summer of 1944 they would launch Operation Capital against the Japanese in Burma. The Allied planners knew that this operation would have a far greater chance of success if it could be combined with an amphibious landing in the Bay of Bengal, but, as General Marshall later explained, "there were not sufficient landing craft to ensure the success of our European offensive and at the same time undertake a landing on the shores of Burma." In Marshall's words, "Victory in this global war depended on the successful execution of Overlord. That must not fail."

One way in which failure would be assured for Overlord was if the Germans could throw into Normandy sufficient divisions to overwhelm the Allied forces, not only on the day of the landings and in the week after that, but even in the month after the landings. To avert this danger, a series of deception plans had been under daily consideration since the previous November, including the unglamorous, uncode-named name Appendix Y, aimed at convincing Hitler that the landings would be in, or east of, the Pas-de-Calais, 140 miles from Normandy. Other deceptions that were put in place in January 1944 depended on the cooperation of the Soviet Union and required Stalin's personal agreement. To secure this, in January 1944 Churchill sent Colonel John Bevan to Moscow together with his American opposite number, Colonel John Baumer. Their expertise was in strategic deception: the art of persuading an enemy that a particular attack was coming, not at its actual point, but somewhere else. They had to convince Stalin that various Soviet military deceptions, as required by the Allies, were essential if Overlord was to succeed.

The deceptions that Bevan and Baumer put to Stalin and his senior military advisers included two major spurious amphibious landings, for which convincing evidence would have to be created for Hitler and the German High Command. One was a Soviet amphibious assault on the Black Sea shore of Romania. The other was a Soviet offensive against northern Norway. Having been convinced by Bevan and Baumer, Stalin agreed to play his part in both these fictional operations. By doing so he ensured that as many as twenty German divisions would be kept away from the Overlord area.

British reading of Ultra—as Enigma had become known—revealed both that Stalin had carried out his promise and that the Germans had fallen for the ruses, as Hitler ordered men and material diverted to the apparently threatened areas.

As Eisenhower and Montgomery set up their respective headquarters in Britain, and an effective, unified command structure, their German adversaries were proving less able to establish a clear chain of command. Rommel, in a substantial enlargement of his earlier responsibilities for the coastal defenses, was appointed to command Army Group B. His new responsibilities extended from Holland to the Atlantic coast of France. Rommel had a plan to repel any invasion; he would use the nine armored divisions of Panzer Group West to hold the area behind the beaches and attack any landing force in the first forty-eight hours. But General Heinz Guderian, Inspector-General of the Armoured Troops, and as such, chief of the Panzer Command, opposed the transfer of any Panzer authority to Rommel. The dispute was taken to Hitler, who decided that Rommel could have authority over only three of the nine divisions. The remainder would be commanded by Rommel's superior, Field Marshal von Rundstedt, Commander-in-Chief, West, but would need Hitler's authority for release.

In further preparation for an invasion that they realized must soon come, the German Armed Forces High Command designated as "fortresses" all the principal ports along both the Atlantic and Channel coasts. Each fortress was given a commander, who took an oath to defend his fortress "to the last round of ammunition, the last can of rations, until every last possibility of defense has been exhausted."

By January 1944 the cross-Channel invasion had become a massive Anglo-American commitment of planning, combining energy and resources, and absorbing the skills of soldiers, sailors, airmen, scientists, and technical experts of all sorts, as well as a formidable Intelligence effort. One element of the preparations ended on January 27, when the

Chief of Staff of the 21st Army Group, Major General Francis de Guingand, called off all further commando raids across the Channel, on the grounds that they served mainly to encourage the Germans to strengthen the coastal defenses yet further.

One commando-type operation was to go ahead. This was the checking of beach gradients and the collection of beach soil samples, a task entrusted to a small unit whose men reached the beaches in midget submarines, the X-Craft. The unit involved was the Combined Operations Pilotage Parties (COPPs). They had first carried out their surreptitious activities in advance of the Torch landings in North Africa. Then, as was also intended for Normandy, they went ashore on the eve of the landing to mark the flanks of the beachhead for the incoming troops, using infra-red beams.

Across Britain, the many elements that were to constitute the invasion force were being gathered, practiced, and prepared in strictest secrecy. The commandos were also dispersed, before D-Day, in twenty-one different locations. (See the map on page 182.)

The planners for the Normandy landings had, at the highest level, to be made privy to material derived from Ultra: from the German top-secret radio messages passing between army, navy, and air headquarters and the regional and local commanders. This was transmitted to Allied commanders-in-chief through Special Liaison Units (SLUs), and these units were at work in both Eisenhower's and Montgomery's headquarters from the last week of January 1944. The information could be substantial, but it also could be fragmentary. Even from the fragments a wider picture could emerge. The first information derived from an Ultra decrypt to reach Eisenhower was sent to him on

January 25. It reported the transfer of some thirty-five German bombers from southern France to the Italian front, a small but welcome piece of news.

On February 1 Montgomery began his second tour of inspection. It took eight days, the general traveling three thousand miles in his personal train, *Rapier,* and speaking to more than 100,000 troops of the 21st Army Group. "This inspection of the men by me, and of me by them," he later wrote, "took some little time, but it was good value for all of us. It was essential that I gained their confidence. I had to begin with their curiosity."

Amphibious training was taking place throughout Britain. (See the map on page 184.) The lessons learned after the Duck I exercise at Slapton Sands encompassed loading and unloading, the number of landing craft required, and the need for specialized gunfire support craft. During the new exercise, Duck II, Rhino ferries—motorized reinforced rafts—were used for the first time to take men and vehicles from the landing craft to the shore.

Despite the careful, wide-ranging preparations, Overlord was cause for daily concern to those who knew of its detailed planning. "The more one goes into it," King George VI wrote in his diary on February 3, "the more alarming it becomes in its vastness."

On February 12 Eisenhower received his formal directive from General Marshall. It began: "You will enter the continent of Europe and, in conjunction with the other United Nations, undertake operations aimed at the heart of Germany and the destruction of her armed forces." Two weeks later, on February 26, Eisenhower issued a top-secret directive about the deception plan designed to convince the

Germans that Normandy was not the Allied destination. The deceptive operations, known since November only as Appendix Y, became Operation Fortitude. One element, Fortitude South, involved the creation in Britain of a vast, spurious military formation, the First United States Army Group, FUSAG. To ensure German belief in it, it was given a commander—the American general, George S. Patton Jr.—bases, training grounds, a communications network, plans, orders of battle, and a specific target, the French coast between Calais and Boulogne, or even, so the Germans were encouraged to believe, farther northeast, on the Belgian and Dutch coasts.

It was not a substantial American force that Patton, one of America's best commanders, commanded in East Anglia, but a vast, deceptive apparatus. The deception worked; the Germans were fooled. Their top agent, Juan Pujol Garcia (known to them as "Arabel"), sent them regular details about the FUSAG plans. He was in fact working for Britain (as "Garbo"), going almost daily to Military Intelligence headquarters in London, where his radio signals and letters to his German spymasters were carefully crafted by his case officer and the deception staff to build up a convincing deception plan.

The Allies did not have access to the German High Command's internal Intelligence summaries, but it was through these that the German war policymakers—and Hitler himself—learned of what the Allies had so desperately wanted them to learn. The first indication (made known to the Allies only after the war) that the Fortitude deception was working was on February 7, when a German Intelligence summary cited "a credible" Army Intelligence source that "has reported the 49th English Infantry Division in the

Norwich-Lowestoft area." The source—in fact another British-controlled agent, "Brutus"—had even located the division's staff as "probably at Beccles," eighteen miles southeast of Norwich. No such division and no such staff headquarters existed, except as part of the paper exercise. On February 17 a German Intelligence summary—quoting Garbo himself, who was described as "a well-regarded source"—said that British and American forces were still in their same areas in East Anglia. On February 18 another German Intelligence summary cited "a good source"— British Intelligence's "Pandora"—to the effect that the 45th English Infantry Division was "stationed in South-Eastern Command." This division was likewise a figment of the British deception planners.

Brutus was a German agent, Roman Garby-Czeriawski, who, on being caught, preferred becoming a double agent to execution. Pandora was not a real person at all, but a creation of British Intelligence, who sent "anonymous" letters from time to time to the senior German diplomat in Dublin, who, it was rightly assumed, would pass them on to German Intelligence in Berlin. His creators portrayed him as a fanatical Irish hater of Britain.

The first indication to reach British Intelligence that the deception was working came in two Ultra messages sent on February 19, in which German troops in the Balkans were ordered from Split to Skopje, and from Mostar to Sarajevo. This was necessary, the top-secret message explained, to be available for rapid movement in the event of an Allied landing in Greece. Further messages, decrypted at Bletchley two weeks later, revealed to the British planners of the Normandy landings that, for the Germans, the First United States Army Group was a reality (see map on page 186).

The phantom army group could therefore continue "threatening" Calais.

Not only was a fictitious United States Army Group to participate in these operations, but also an equally fictitious British Twelfth Army, containing, among its forces, the 15th British Motorized Division, the 34th British Infantry Division, the 8th British Armored Division, and the 7th Polish Infantry Division, all apparently equipped, deployed, moved, trained, and communicated with, and yet existing only on paper.

A separate deception army was set up in Scotland, intended to give verisimilitude to an Allied amphibious landing on the coast of Norway. German Intelligence worked hard to identify as many of its units as possible, and it succeeded in locating, among entirely fictional units, the First Norwegian Army, the 12th Norwegian Infantry Brigade, the 2nd Polish Infantry Division, the Polish Parachute Brigade, two American Infantry Divisions, and a British Army Corps. (See the map on page 187.)

It was by reading Germany's own top-secret messages that the Combined Chiefs of Staff would know whether the Germans had been taken in by Fortitude and by the other deceptions that were intended to ensure the widest possible dispersion of German forces by a skillfully leaked set of eight separate British landings. Each of these landings was a figment of the imagination, and deception skills, of the London Controlling Section under Colonel Bevan. As well as Fortitude South, pointing to the Pas-de-Calais as the cross-Channel destination, there was Fortitude North against central Norway, centered on Trondheim; Operation Graffham, against central Sweden; Operation Royal Flush, against the coastlines of three neutral countries: Sweden,

Spain, or Turkey; Operation Zeppelin, a triple assault against the Romanian Black Sea coast, Crete, and the western coastline of Greece and Albania; Operation Ironside against Bordeaux; Operation Vendetta, against Marseille; and Operation Ferdinand against Rome. (See the map on page 191.)

A careful scrutiny at Bletchley of the Ultra decrypts revealed just how seriously the Germans were taking these nonexistent threats. Reports had been received, Churchill told General Sir Maitland Wilson, Commander-in-Chief of the British forces in the Mediterranean, "that the islands off the Dalmatian coast are being equipped with naval guns." Churchill's telegram was dated February 13; Ultra was his source.

On February 20, British and American bombers launched Operation Argument, a week-long series of massive attacks, also known as "Big Week," against German aircraft and ball-bearing factories and port installations within the substantial triangle Brussels–Rostock–Pola. (See the map on page 185.)

On the first night of the Anglo-American "Big Week" raids, the Germans were also bombing London; four people were killed just outside the Prime Minister's residence at 10 Downing Street, although Churchill himself was out of London that night. Returning to London two days later, he revealed to the House of Commons that, since the beginning of the war, 38,300 British pilots and aircrew had been killed, and 10,000 aircraft lost. Britain's most recent four raids, including the one on Leipzig, "constitute," he said, "the most violent attacks which have yet been made on Germany, and they also prove the value of saturation in every aspect of the air war." The air offensive, he added, "constitutes the foundation upon which our plans for overseas invasion stand."

Much of the damage done during "Big Week" was quickly repaired. At Augsburg, the main aircraft factory was back in full production in little more than a month. Whereas the average German monthly production of single-engine fighters was 851 in the last half of 1943, it rose to a monthly average of 1,581 in the first half of 1944. But although Germany's aircraft factories continued to produce substantial numbers of aircraft, this productivity was not matched by the training of sufficient pilots.

For the Americans, the losses during "Big Week" were considerable, with 2,600 crewmen killed in action, seriously wounded, or taken prisoner.

At the request of the Ministry of Supply, Montgomery visited factories all over Britain whose workers were producing equipment for the troops. On February 22, at Euston Station, he spoke to a gathering of railwaymen from throughout Britain whose task would be to move vast numbers of troops and quantities of supplies as the day of the cross-Channel assault drew near. "I spoke for an hour and a half," he later recalled, "and told them of our problems in what lay ahead and how they could help. I said we now had the war in a very good grip, and the bad days were over; we must rally to the task and finish the war."

On March 3, again at the request of the Ministry of Supply, Montgomery went to the London Docks, where he spoke to 16,000 dockers, stevedores, and lightermen who manned the barges, all of whose work was essential to the invasion preparations.

To increase the number of commandos available for the

landings, a new unit, No. 48 Royal Marine Commando, was formed on March 4, and sent to Achnacarry in Scotland—within sight of Britain's highest mountain, Ben Nevis—where they underwent an intensive three months' training.

Throughout Britain the munitions factories were working at fullest capacity. "I stood on a bridge one day," recalled Melvyn Greene, then a nine-year-old schoolboy, "and saw the largest train I had ever seen pass slowly by packed with tanks. I thought it would go on forever."

On March 4, in Moscow, Soviet Intelligence and military experts gave their approval to the Anglo-American deception plans for the Normandy landings. Fictitious Soviet military activity would make its contribution to the Allied plan for a spurious landing on the coast of Norway. By a coincidence of timing, March 4 also was the day on which a German Intelligence document, discussing Allied plans for the "decisive Atlantic front," noted that the Allied strategists, having been "successful" in the creation of an active "subsidiary front" in Italy, might have come "to a like decision in the Scandinavian area."

On March 5 Eisenhower moved his headquarters out of London and away from the center of government in Whitehall. He wanted somewhere less accessible to the hustle and bustle of the capital. He chose Bushey Park, near Hampton Court, some fifteen miles from Whitehall. The new Supreme Headquarters was given the code name Widewing. Eisenhower's personal accommodation was just under a mile away, across the Thames, at Telegraph Cottage in Kingston-upon-Thames.

At the highest level of German planning, the Anglo-

American deception plans were working well. On March 5 the Supreme Command of the German Navy (OKM) reported that there might be as many as six British divisions in Scotland ready for an operation "of limited scope" against central and southern Norway. This top-secret signal, decrypted at Bletchley, revealed to the Allies that the Fortitude North deception plan was working. No such operation against the Germans in Norway was planned.

On the night of March 6, in preparation for the Normandy landings, then only three months away at most, 263 British bombers dropped more than a thousand tons of bombs on the railway center at Trappes, just west of Paris. Tracks, engine sheds, engines, and railway wagons were so badly damaged that the center was unable to function for more than a month. During that month, eight other rail centers in northern France were attacked with similar effect.

At the beginning of March, the issue of security came to the fore in the most secret counsels of those planning the landings. Strongly encouraged to do so by Montgomery, on March 6 Eisenhower wrote to the British Chiefs of Staff that "it would go hard with our consciences if we were to feel . . . that by neglecting any security precaution we had compromised the success of these vital operations or need-lessly squandered men's lives." Three days later the Home Defence Committee of the British War Cabinet agreed to a far more stringent ban than the earlier one. The new ban would prevent 600,000 visitors a month from traveling to the towns and coastal areas along the North Sea, the English Channel, and the Bristol Channel.

One hundred percent censorship of the mails was imposed on all correspondence with Northern Ireland—

hitherto a source of leakage through neutral Eire. Mail to all foreign countries and to Gibraltar was subjected to an artificial delay of thirty days between its mailing and dispatch overseas. Mail to British prisoners of war in Germany, a particularly vulnerable route for sensitive information, was subjected to a three-month delay. The Swedish air service between Aberdeen and neutral Sweden was "interrupted."

In Britain, Eisenhower was steadily building up his contacts and authority. On March 11 he visited No. 100 Officer Cadet Training unit at Britain's Royal Military Academy, at Sandhurst. Before reviewing the passing-out parade, he spoke to the nineteen- and twenty-year-old British officer-cadets, many of whom would be going into battle under his command within the next three months. "You young men have this war to win," he told them. It was "small-unit leadership" that was going to win the ground battle, a battle that had to be won before "that enemy of ours is finally crushed."

His wish, Eisenhower told the young officers, was: "If I could only meet you all somewhere east of the Rhine and renew the acquaintance of this morning." His final words were: "Good Luck."

Three days after Eisenhower's visit to Sandhurst, Rommel was at Les Petites Dalles on the Channel coast between Le Havre and Dieppe—at the very spot where on 10 June 1940 he had reached the Channel coast with the conquering German army. He was making a second major inspection of the Atlantic Wall defenses. At the same time, Heinrich Himmler, head of the SS, was evolving a scheme that would have averted a cross-Channel landing altogether. On March 20, General William J. Donovan, Director of the Office of Strategic Services (the OSS), informed Roosevelt that he had received a message from neutral Sweden that Himmler was contemplating the overthrow of Hitler, to be followed by negotiations between himself and the Allies, with a view to ending the war in the West and forming a joint German-American-British war front against the Soviet Union.

Roosevelt at once contacted Churchill. Both men agreed that the offer must be rejected out of hand. The Allied policy of Unconditional Surrender would remain in force. The Soviet Union was the Eastern ally and would remain so until the whole Nazi apparatus—including Himmler and the SS—had been destroyed.

Having completed his second tour of the Atlantic Wall defenses, Rommel was summoned on March 19—with all the leading Field Marshals—to Berchtesgaden, traveling to southern Bavaria from his headquarters at la Roche-Guyon. The result of the visit was a "thought piece" by Hitler, dated March 20, in which he suggested that the two most threatened areas were the Brest and Cotentin Peninsulas, "which are very tempting and offer the best possibilities for the formation of a bridgehead, which would then be enlarged systematically by the mass use of air forces and heavy weapons of all kinds." The most westerly American beachhead, at Utah Beach, was at the base of the Cotentin Peninsula. But Hitler thought the attack would come, as it had done at Dieppe, against a port; in the case of the Cotentin Peninsula, against Cherbourg itself.

Hitler's assessment, although incorrect, was less wide of the mark than that of the Intelligence Department of the German Armed Forces High Command (OKW). Also on

March 20 they presented Hitler with their conclusions—in a top-secret radio signal decrypted at Bletchley. The OKW Intelligence Department located the area of the landings as "somewhere between the Pas-de-Calais and the Loire Valley"—that is, both the Channel coast and part of the Atlantic coast of France.

Another German signal, decrypted three days later and giving comfort to the Allied planners, was the first to mention General Patton as the commander of the First United States Army Group—the fictional force preparing in East Anglia to land at the Pas-de-Calais or farther northeast, 120 miles from the actual landing beaches.

6

The Mounting Costs

Trouble loomed in the Anglo-American camp in the third week of March. It centered on a conflict among the air commanders. On March 22 Eisenhower was so distressed by their disagreements that he sent General Marshall a resignation threat. "The air problem has been one requiring a great deal of patience and negotiations," Eisenhower wrote. "Unless the matter is settled at once I will request relief from this command."

The issue was a clash of both personalities and priorities, between tactical aviation—using the bombers to strike at German positions and lines of communication in France—and strategic aviation, using the bombers against the German homeland, to defeat Germany without the need for a major confrontation on land. The head of Bomber Command, Air Chief Marshal Sir Arthur Harris, believed that the best way to weaken Germany was by concentrating the whole weight of Allied bombing power on Germany. Harris was supported in his view by General Carl Spaatz, the commander of the United States Strategic Air Forces in Europe (USSTAF), administratively responsible for the Ninth Air Force, whose sixteen hundred American P-47 fighters were based in Britain. Spaatz, who thought the Normandy landings were not only unnecessary but also doomed to failure, expressed his feelings in a blunt question to a senior colleague: "Why undertake a highly dubious operation when there is a sure way to do it?" That sure way was bombing the German homeland.

Eisenhower wanted the Ninth Air Force fighter-bombers to focus their main effort on attacking German military targets in France in advance of the invasion and as a crucial preliminary to it. He was supported by Air Chief Marshal Sir Trafford Leigh-Mallory, the British airman he had chosen to command the Allied Expeditionary Air Force, and by the Deputy Supreme Commander, Sir Arthur Tedder, who, also under Eisenhower, had earlier commanded the Allied air forces in the Mediterranean.

At a conference with all the air commanders on March 25, Eisenhower demanded a decision without delay. Spaatz pressed for the "Oil Offensive," a massive attack against German oil storage and transit facilities. Tedder pressed for the "Transportation Plan," an equally massive assault that had already begun against all seventy-six German rail centers and rail repair shops in France designated by Professor Solly Zuckerman.

Tedder used in his support a paper by his scientific adviser, Zuckerman, who argued that if the seventy-six most important rail servicing and repair facilities in northwestern Europe were destroyed, it would "paralyze movements in the whole region they serve and render almost impossible the subsequent movement by rail of major reserves into France." The advocates—and the needs—of tactical bombing won the argument. On March 26 Eisenhower approved the continuation of the Transportation Plan.

Within three weeks, control of the strategic bomber forces was transferred to Eisenhower's headquarters, ensuring that the Transportation Plan would receive the highest priority. During some sixteen weeks, 21,949 sorties were carried out, and 66,517 tons of bombs dropped: an average of 190 sorties and 568 tons of bombs each day. The attacks were carried out by the planes of the Allied Expeditionary Air Force, Royal Air Force Coastal Command, and the United States Eighth Air Force. In the attack on Courtrai, March 26–27, more than 250 Belgians lost their lives; many of the dead were visitors to the town who had come to celebrate that Sunday's religious festival.

During these attacks, many of them in or near city centers, several thousand civilians were killed. At a conference on April 5, Churchill expressed his unease at the heavy loss of civilian life—the captive peoples whom the Allies were soon to try to liberate—but Eisenhower did not feel he could risk any German troops and munitions reaching the battlefield after the landings if there was the slightest chance of preventing them in advance. Once the battle had begun, it might be too late, as the fighter-bombers would be needed for direct tactical support over the battlefield.

On March 30 another indispensable component of the cross-Channel assault was created, IX Engineer Command. Its task would be to build landing grounds and airfields as soon as land was under Allied control, as close to the front line as possible. By the day of the landings the command would have more than 17,000 members. In the first three weeks of the battle, as a result of their engineering skills, more than that number of wounded men (a total of 19,490) were to be evacuated by air to Britain.

On April 1, two days after the creation of IX Engineer

Command, an essential Allied air reconnaissance plan was begun under the Central Reconnaissance Committee at Eisenhower's headquarters. It was to be a crucial element of the landings themselves. One of its aims was to prepare sea-level photographs—known as "wavetop" obliques—of the coastline along which the Allied forces would land. To prevent any German alert as to the actual destinations, the whole coastline from Holland to the Spanish frontier was covered, an enormous task for the aircrews. As well as the sea-level photographs, other obliques were taken showing both the landing beaches and the terrain inland. Higher-altitude obliques covered the inland areas from different angles.

Beach defenses, beach gradients, and the ever-expanding coastal defenses of the Atlantic Wall were all covered in detail. Bridges, and riverbanks where bridges would have to be built, were two other objectives for these photographic flights. Engineers studied the photographs to select the locations of airfields that would have to be constructed in the first days after the landing.

Between April 1 and June 5, planes of the Allied Expeditionary Air Force flew 3,215 photographic reconnaissance sorties. Aircraft of other commands, including Royal Air Force Coastal Command and the United States Eighth Air Force, flew a further 1,519 reconnaissance sorties. These sorties averaged just over seventy a day.

On April 4, a rehearsal for the day of the Allied cross-Channel invasion was carried out using live ammunition. The exercise was given the code name Smash. Held at Studland Bay, in Dorset, it involved the launching, in darkness, of the amphibious DD (Duplex Drive, known colloquially as Donald Duck) tank, designed to propel itself from the landing craft to the shore as a boat and then to proceed on land as a tank. The tanks were launched 5,000 yards offshore. The exercise was realistic to the point of danger: seven tanks sank and six men were drowned.

The intensity of the training and the need for secrecy affected the whole of Britain. On April 6 all leaves were canceled for all troops who would be involved in the coming landings. In France, the British effort to sustain and stimulate the French Resistance was continuous. Also on April 6 a French-Canadian from Montreal, Jean-Paul Archambault, was parachuted into France near Lyon.

As an agent of Britain's Special Operations Executive (SOE), Archambault helped to form three groups of local saboteurs. One, in the Bourges area, consisted of 250 members. For Eisenhower, as Supreme Commander, and for Montgomery, as Commander-in-Chief, whatever disruption could be made to the movement of German troops and supplies in France added a welcome element of strength.

The Germans responded with alacrity. On April 7, German troops moved against French Resistance fighters in the hills around Gex and Oyonnax, in the Jura Mountains. Code-named Operation Spring, the sweep involved six German regiments and a regiment of Cossacks—Soviet citizens who, having been taken prisoner of war in southern Russia in 1941 and 1942, had volunteered to fight for the Germans.

On the first day of the sweep, five members of the Resistance were killed and thirteen captured. That same week, in northern France, near Angers, German agents captured twenty Frenchmen who, a month earlier, had pieced together for the British a detailed fifty-five-foot map of the

German defenses in the Cotentin Peninsula, on the eastern edge of which a part of the cross-Channel invasion was to take place, and had managed to arrange for it to be smuggled back to Britain. All twenty were executed when the invasion began.

As the bombing campaign of the Transportation Plan was about to go into full gear, several preliminary attacks on German rail facilities in France showed that the civilian cost would be high. On the night of April 9–10 the targets were two railway yards, one at Lille, and the other at Villeneuve-St-Georges, near Paris. At Villeneuve more than ninety civilians were killed. At Lille, where most of the bombs fell on a residential suburb, 456 civilians were killed.

The next evening, Eisenhower left by train from London with two of his air force commanders, General Spaatz and General Brereton, for a tour of American air bases in East Anglia. During their tour, they were shown "strike photos" of earlier attacks on three railway yards in France: at Creil, Hasselt, and Haine-St-Pierre. They also watched a group take off for a bombing raid on the railway yards at Charleroi, in Belgium.

The parachuting of British agents into France continued. On the night of April 8–9 Muriel Byck, code name Violette, was parachuted in to join the Ventriloquist (Special Operations Executive/French Resistance) circuit, based south of Orléans. Its task, when the cross-Channel landings came, was to block the railway cuttings in its area. Violette was to die of meningitis a month later, before Ventriloquist's work was called for.

Along the area of the Atlantic Wall, the Germans were putting up antiairborne landing poles (many of them the trunks of trees that had been cut down to improve the line of fire of gun batteries) in all fields that seemed to offer a possible landing place for Allied gliders and parachutists. These obstacles became known to the troops who were to encounter them as "Rommel's asparagus." On April 17, as part of this wide-ranging scheme, they were being erected around Sainte-Mère-Église, at the very focal point of one of the planned dropping zones of the American parachutists supporting the Utah Beach landings. Also that day an order was given for all the townspeople to hand in their radios. There would be "severe penalties" for anyone listening to the BBC.

On April 14, the head of Bomber Command, Air Chief Marshal Sir Arthur Harris, who was certain that Germany would be defeated through the bombing of German industry, accepted that even his Operation Pointblank—the day and night bombing of Germany—had to concede priority to Overlord. From that moment, Eisenhower was the ultimate arbiter of how the Anglo-American air forces in Britain would be used and where they would strike.

At midnight on April 17–18 the most controversial preinvasion security measure, considered essential by the British security planners, was put into force. The diplomatic representatives of all neutral countries were forbidden to send or receive uncensored communications, whether by diplomatic bag or cipher. Movement of diplomatic couriers, and all other diplomatic personnel, was banned. This applied not only to neutral but also to Allied diplomats, with the exception of the Soviet Union and the United States.

.   .   .

There was a setback for Hitler that week when the Turkish government declared on April 20—Hitler's fifty-fifth birthday—that it would no longer send chrome to Germany. The Soviet reconquest of the Crimea made it dangerous for Turkey to continue with her absolute neutrality; now, more than a year after Churchill had gone specially to Adana in southern Turkey to try to persuade the Turks to enter the war, it was announced that Turkey was no longer a neutral but a "pro-Allied" nation—though not a belligerent.

As of April 1944, Germany's stocks of chrome were sufficient for no more than a year and a half's further production of the high-grade steel needed to manufacture tanks. Yet Hitler had hopes that new tanks, faster and more powerful—some of which were demonstrated to him on April 20 at Klessheim Castle, just outside Salzburg—could halt the Soviet thrust on the Eastern Front and check any cross-Channel invasion at the shore. Yet the Security Police "Report from the Reich" of April 20 stated unequivocably that "developments in the East and the continually deferred hope of 'a saving miracle' are gradually producing signs of weariness among the people."

Hitler had no inkling that one of his own most top secret Ultra messages, setting out the western itinerary of General Guderian as Inspector-General of Panzer Troops, had not only enabled the German tank commanders to prepare for the visit, but also had given British Intelligence, who also read it, a clear picture of the location and distribution of Germany's armored forces, less than two months before the Normandy landing was due to take place.

The first lap of Guderian's itinerary was the tank headquarters at Mailly-le-Camp, near Reims. Even as Guderian moved on to his next stop, at Amiens, British bombers struck at Mailly-le-Camp, killing as many as a hundred soldiers and injuring many more.* But it was not always the Germans who suffered from the intensification of Allied bombing over France that month. When, on April 21, a heavy night raid over Paris struck at the marshaling yard of St-Denis and the Gare de la Chapelle, 640 Parisians were killed.

The growing number of German divisions known through Ultra to be in northwestern France was causing alarm among the Allied leaders. But Intelligence also was able to show that their actual strength was not excessive and that the scale of German strength needed to postpone or cancel D-Day would not be reached. Guderian's journey had helped to confirm this.

Rommel was confident that he could defeat any invasion force, writing on April 23 to General Alfred Jodl, Chief of the Operations Staff of the German Armed Forces High Command (OKW): "If, in spite of the enemy's air superiority, we succeed in getting a large part of our mobile force into action in the threatened coast defense sectors in the first few hours, I am convinced that the enemy attack on the coast will collapse completely on its first day." Rommel added, ominously for the Allies: "Very little damage has so far been done by the heavy enemy bombing to our reinforced concrete installation"—although "our field positions, dugouts, and communication trenches have in many places been completely obliterated."

In the same potential battle area, it was French civilians

*For a map of Guderian's journey, as revealed to the British through Ultra, see page 189.

who had begun to suffer that spring, as Allied bombers carried out the Transportation Plan for the destruction of German railway yards and junctions throughout the Normandy, Seine, and Pas-de-Calais regions. On April 24, four hundred people were killed during an American daylight raid on the railway yards at Rouen, when many bombs fell on the center of the city.

Throughout the spring of 1944 Churchill held regular meetings with Eisenhower and his Chief of Staff, General Bedell Smith. Together the three men examined every aspect of the landing preparations, including the initial airborne assault, the naval bombardment, and air cover. Headquarters staffs were moving closer to the embarkation points. On April 26 Admiral Sir Bertram Ramsay, Naval Commander for Overlord, set up his headquarters just outside Portsmouth, at Southwick House. Ramsay was responsible for the sea transportation and landing phases of Overlord, which were given their own code name, Neptune. A major decision still to be made by Ramsay and Eisenhower was at what hour the landings should take place. The exact date was yet to be decided.

The original month for the cross-Channel landings had been May. The postponement by a month was needed, above all, to complete the intricate work of creating the two artificial harbors, code-named Mulberry, which would avoid the Dieppe example of having to attack an existing, fortified, harbor. Among the components of each Mulberry were three that lay at its core. The first were breakwaters to protect the harbors, which would be made by sinking seventy old naval and merchant ships in a great arc around them. These were the breakwater ships given the code name

Gooseberry. They were both to serve as the outer ring of the two Mulberry harbors, and as independent breakwaters on their own, at other beaches.

The harbors themselves would be made up of roadway units, code-named Whales, and a harbor itself, consisting of 146 enormous watertight caissons of steel and concrete, code-named Phoenix. The largest Phoenix caissons weighed more than 6,000 tons. They required 600,000 tons of concrete (the weight of more than two thousand two-storey houses) and a million and a half yards of steel shuttering. To build them, 20,000 men were employed, working in eight dry docks, two wet docks, and twelve enormous holes excavated next to the River Thames, below water level, with a barrier of earth between them and the Thames; the barrier was breached when the Phoenix was ready to float into the river. Not only did they have to float, but also, once off the Normandy coast—to which they would be towed by tug— they had to sink, and sink swiftly, to form the harbor wall. That sinking time, originally 1½ hours, was reduced by practice to 22 minutes.

The Mulberry task was assigned to Rear Admiral W. G. Tennant, who, as a naval captain, had helped supervise the evacuation of the Dunkirk beaches. For the Mulberries, Tennant had a staff of 500 officers and 10,000 men, working as part of four separate but interlinking organizations: the Build-Up Control Organization (BUCO), the Turn Round Control Organization (TURCO), the Control Repair Organization (COREP), and the Control Tug Organization (COTUG). Behind the acronyms lay a massive effort by sailors, engineers, and mechanics in the two months leading up to D-Day.

.   .   .

More than a hundred small-scale parachute and land actions were also part of the D-Day plan. For each of these, preparations were being made at locations throughout Britain. Among those devised and practiced in April was the capture, by the 9th Parachute Battalion, of the Merville Battery, on the eastern flank of the British landings. This was an objective that had been included in the plan by Montgomery. It was an essential prelude to the seaborne landings.

Seven hundred men were to take part in the assault of the Merville Battery, fifty of them in gliders. The commander of the battalion, Lieutenant Colonel Terence Otway, whose men often found him a hard taskmaster, worked with them at a farm near Netheravon to perfect the capture, using a scale model of the battery. This did not satisfy him, and he decided to build a full-scale model elsewhere. To do this, he was given a forty-five-acre site on Walbury Hill, near Newbury, where men of the Royal Engineers worked with bulldozers for seven days and nights to reproduce the anti-tank ditch, the paths, the gun emplacements and the minefield areas.

Practice seaborne landings were taking place on various beaches in southern England. The largest of these exercises, Operation Tiger, was carried out at Slapton Sands between April 26 and 28. It was intended as the final rehearsal for the American troops who would land on Utah Beach (Assault Force U). Their escorting destroyer, HMS *Scimitar*, the main escort for the convoy, had been in a collision with a landing craft the night before and did not sail from Plymouth after her repairs.

As the exercise proceeded, seven German torpedo boats, which were on a routine night patrol from Cherbourg, came across Operation Tiger while it was at sea. Two of the eight

Tank landing ships were torpedoed and sunk and another was badly damaged. There was considerable loss of life—kept secret at the time—with 639 American soldiers killed. This was three times the number who would die on Utah Beach on D-Day.

For mounting the attack, the German commander of the naval patrol, Captain Rudolf Peterson, was awarded the much-prized Oak Leaves to the Knight's Cross which he had won in 1940. Rear Admiral Don P. Moon, the American commander of Assault Force U, committed suicide three months later. The Commander-in-Chief, Plymouth, Admiral Sir Ralph Leatham, while admitting a "lack of liaison" with regard to the absent destroyer, pointed out that the Royal Navy was about to carry out a major offensive operation in the Channel on April 28 and that "the capacity of the staff was severely stretched."

Many of the dead Americans were specialist engineers who could not easily be replaced. Ten of the American officers drowned off Slapton Sands on April 28 had secret information relevant to the actual cross-Channel invasion—information given under the code name Bigot only to those who needed to know it. To ensure that none of the ten had been picked up at sea by the Germans—who had taken several men prisoner—a vast search was carried out, and all the corpses that could be recovered were carefully examined. Although more than a hundred bodies were never recovered, those of each of the ten Bigot officers were found. The cross-Channel secrets remained safe.

7

The Month of May

On 1 May 1944, General Eisenhower and Admiral Ramsay examined evidence, including aerial photographs and agents' reports, of the strengthening of the Atlantic Wall, and in particular the obstacles that were being put in place below the high-water mark. As a result of Rommel's cleverly designed improvements to the coastal defenses, Eisenhower and Ramsay decided that the landings would take place in daylight, and at low tide, so that the underwater obstacles would be visible and avoidable.

Mines also were features of the German underwater defenses. These mines led to No. 10 Inter-Allied Commando mounting a small but clever deception exercise, code-named Tarbrush. Sailing from Dover in motor torpedo boats, the commandos went ashore in the Pas-de-Calais area, leaving subtle clues that they had been there examining the beach defenses, to make the Pas-de-Calais appear as the intended landing area. The Tarbrush operations also had a nondeception aspect. While ashore they were able to check the general method and location of the mine belts and to examine the different types of mines being used for beach defenses. They found five types: magnetic, contact, acoustic, electrically controlled, and mines activated by the entry of seawater.

The first Tarbrush operation sailed on May 14, followed by seven more over the next four days. On each crossing, three commandos went ashore. Those of Tarbrush 3 carried out their examination of the beach despite a man smoking a cigarette 150 yards from their landing point. The three members of Tarbrush 8, who spent an hour and a half ashore, were able to confirm that there were no mines between the obstacle belt and the low-water line. This meant that troops landing at low tide would not have to deal with mines before they reached the obstacles, but only closer to shore.

The final exercises for the Normandy landings were held in the first week of May and code-named Fabius. The rehearsal for Assault Force O, the Americans who would land on Omaha Beach, began on May 2. It was held off Slapton Sands, scene of the April disaster, and lasted five days. On May 3 the two British assault forces, Assault Force S (for Sword Beach) and Assault Force G (for Gold Beach), carried out their full and final rehearsals west of Littlehampton and on Hayling Island, respectively. Assault Force J (for Juno Beach), the Canadians, also had their final practice that week, east of Brackelsham Bay.

An array of vessels was involved in these practices, as in the real landings. The Americans emerged principally from their Higgins Boats; their official name was Landing Craft, Vehicle/Personnel, or LCVP, designed, as were several other specialized craft, by Andrew Higgins of New Orleans. The British emerged from their Landing Craft, Assault

(LCA). These landing craft were light enough, at ten tons, to be slung on the davits of converted passenger ships and ferries for the duration of the Channel crossing. Each held thirty-eight men, and once "launched" from the parent ship they could move forward at seven to ten knots. There were also the LCIs (Landing Craft, Infantry).

Above France and Belgium, the bombers of the Transportation Plan were wreaking havoc on German railway yards and railway repair facilities. But they were also killing many civilians. On the night of May 1–2, a total of 171 Belgians were killed during the raid on Malines. Their fate led to the plan being suspended while Churchill sought an assurance that no raid would be carried out that would result in the death of more than a hundred civilians. At a Defence Committee meeting on May 3, Air Marshal Tedder argued that this would mean a serious curtailment of the plan, but Churchill was not convinced that civilian casualties were merited, telling Tedder, "You will smear the good name of the Royal Air Force across the world."

It was decided to put the matter to Roosevelt. Members of the War Cabinet, Churchill informed the President, were unanimous in their anxieties about "these French slaughters," even on a "reduced scale," and sought his guidance. Roosevelt took a decisive view, telling Churchill, "However regrettable the attendant loss of civilian life is, I am not prepared to impose from this distance any restriction on military action by the responsible commanders that in their opinion might militate against the success of Overlord or cause additional loss of life to our Allied forces of invasion."

Roosevelt's view was accepted, and the Transportation Plan went ahead. Some raids killed hardly any civilians. But on the night of May 12–13, some 160 Belgians were killed at Louvain, and sixteen days later, on the night of May 28–29, an estimated 254 French civilians were killed at Angers.

The Allies continued to use the Germans' own top-secret Ultra radio messages to refine their invasion plans. On May 3 a newly formed German division reached France. Four days later, as a result of reading the German army's Ultra signals, the Anglo-American planners knew not only of its existence but also of its strength—defensive only—and location, at the base of the Cotentin Peninsula.

The order had been given by Hitler, direct to Rommel, to strengthen the Normandy coast and the area around Cherbourg, specifically against airborne landings. Hitler judged, rightly, that Cherbourg would be an objective of any such landing in that area. Rommel moved the 91st Division from its base in Nantes to the very area of the Cotentin Peninsula that was intended (unknown to the Germans) to be one of the American dropping zones. Ultra enabled the Allied planners to follow the movement with precision and to adjust their own landing plans accordingly. Of this, the Germans knew nothing.

Thus the most secret triumph of British Intelligence, and the hard, often laborious work of more than five thousand cryptographers and their helpers, reached a high point of achievement, averting all danger of a "blind" landing in France. One by one, each German military formation was precisely located.

On May 5, in a success for their own Intelligence services, the Germans were able to eavesdrop on a telephone conversation between Churchill and Roosevelt. Something was in preparation, but what it was, or where, or when, they could neither overhear nor deduce. Particularly galling for those who read the transcript of the discussion were Roosevelt's final words: "Well, we will do our best—now I'll go fishing."

In Western Europe the planning and deception for Overlord were in their final month. For some time Montgomery had been pressing for air attacks on the railway bridges across the Seine below Paris, and across the Loire below Orléans, bridges that would have to be used by the Germans to move men and materials to the battlefield. When the bombing experts estimated that 1,200 tons of bombs would be needed to ensure the destruction of a single bridge, Air Chief Marshal Sir Trafford Leigh-Mallory felt obliged to turn the request down as too costly. But the American head of IX Fighter Command, Major General Elwood R. Quesada, prevailed upon Leigh-Mallory to let him try. He would do it, he said, with his P-47 fighter aircraft, each with a single ton of bombs.

On May 7 the Interdiction Plan was put into action. That day, eight Thunderbolt fighter-bombers flew along the River Seine to the railway bridge at Vernon, thirty-five miles from Paris—and only a few miles from Rommel's headquarters at la Roche-Guyon. Each plane, flying below the height of the bridge, released two 1,000-pound bombs as it pulled up abruptly, sending the bombs into the bridge abutments. Sixteen bombs, with a total weight of eight tons, cut the bridge in half. Three days later, Leigh-Mallory authorized a full-scale attack against the Seine bridges.

Of the eighty rail targets selected, fifty-one were judged to be too badly damaged by D-Day to require further attack. Almost all the rest were reported by air reconnaissance to be "very severely damaged," but with some facilities still requiring further attack. Only four of the targets were reported to have suffered little or no damage. Destruction of the bridges across the Loire was left until after D-Day, to avoid too obvious a definition of the Allied assault area. (See the map on page 190.)

No date had yet been selected for the landings. Eisenhower and his senior colleagues and staff, meeting at Supreme Headquarters, studied the weather, moon, and tides. On May 8 they came to a decision. The next group of days on which a landing would be possible in optimum conditions would be June 5, 6, and 7. They selected June 5.

Rommel, summoned to a high-level conference in Paris on May 8, urged von Rundstedt to allow him to be in direct command of the four first-class armored (Panzer) divisions. These included three SS Panzer Divisions, which the Armed Forces High Command—the OKW—was keeping as a centralized reserve under its own direct command. Rommel's appeal was not successful. From Paris he returned to his headquarters and then, without a break, continued to the coast, resuming his ever-vigilant watch over the daily strengthening of defenses.

The Germans were making every effort to try to estimate when and where an Anglo-American assault would come. On May 8 von Rundstedt sent his superiors an estimate that the Allied preparations were complete and that twenty divisions would be landed in the first wave. This was four times the number of divisions then preparing for the first assault. Von Rundstedt also reported, on the basis of his Intelligence information, that the main concentration of troops preparing for the assault was between Southampton and Portsmouth. This was reasonably accurate, but his attempt to locate the landing areas was far from precise: somewhere, he said, between the mouth of the River Scheldt (the port of Antwerp) and the Atlantic coast of Brittany, but most probably "between Boulogne and Normandy." It would be essential, von Rundstedt concluded, for the Allies to capture large ports like Cherbourg and Le Havre. A week after von Rundstedt sent this estimate, it was decrypted at Bletchley and sent to Eisenhower and Montgomery. Neither Cherbourg nor Le Havre were D-Day objectives.

A German Air Force signal, sent on May 8 and decrypted at Bletchley that same day, forecast that the landings would be between Le Havre and Cherbourg. This was the most accurate of all the German Intelligence forecasts at that time. It was reflected on May 9, when Rommel inspected the heavy gun positions along the Channel coast and on the Cotentin Peninsula (see the bottom map on page 189), writing in his diary, "Drive to the Cotentin Peninsula, which seems to have become the focal point of the invasion."

It was a strenuous journey, taking Rommel first to Houlgate (six miles east of the Merville Battery objective) and then to Caen, where he was given a briefing by his senior commanders. After lunch in Caen he toured the exact area of what were to be Gold, Juno, and Sword Beaches, followed by a visit to the fortified naval battery at le Chaos. From there he went to inspect the St-Marcouf battery at Crisbecq, where repairs and extensions had repeatedly been disrupted by Allied air attacks. Work on this battery had begun in 1941. It was one of the first constructions of the Todt Organization, and it had a clear field of fire over what was soon to be Utah Beach. But at the time of Rommel's visit only two of its four guns were protected by concrete casemates.

During his visit to the Utah Beach area, Rommel visited Blockhouse W5, part of the Atlantic Wall defenses. Major and Mrs. Holt, in their description of the museum that was built many years later around the blockhouse, write, "When Rommel was pleased with what he found he often gave a concertina or mouth-organ to one of the soldiers putting up obstacles, in the hope that the soldier would play and encourage his comrades to sing, thus building morale. When he came here, however, he was not pleased. He inspected the beach and the obstacles, and then demanded that Lieutenant Arthur Jahnke, in charge of Blockhouse W5, take off his gloves and show his palms. Jahnke did so and, on seeing the weals and scratches on the young officer's hands, which had clearly come from helping to put up beach obstacles, Rommel relented and told him that the blood he had spilled in putting up obstacles was as important as any he would spill in combat."

Rommel then continued via Grandcamp and Isigny to St-Lô, where he dined. His route had taken him through much of the area where the landings would come and where the fighting would be most severe. He was under no illusion about how formidable his adversaries would be. In a private talk with his former Chief of Staff (in North Africa), General Fritz Bayerlein, Rommel expressed his anxieties about the refusal of the Armed Forces High Command to let him have control of the four reserve Panzer divisions. "Our friends in the East," he said—the generals fighting on the Russian Front, whose influence was strong in Berlin—"cannot imagine what they are in for here. It is not a matter of fanatical hordes to be driven forward in masses against our line, with no regard for casualties and little recourse to tactical craft; here we are facing an enemy who applies all his native intelligence to the use of his many technical recourses; who spares no expenditure of material and whose very operation goes its course as though it had been the subject of repeated rehearsal. Dash and doggedness alone no longer make a soldier. He must have sufficient intelligence to enable him to get the most out of his fighting machine. And that is something the Anglo-Americans can do—we found that out in North Africa."

On the day of Rommel's journey to what was to be the future battlefield, American bombers struck at the principal German airfields in northwestern Europe: at Laon, Florennes, Thionville, St-Dizier, Juvincourt, Orléans, and Avord. (See the map on page 188.) That same day, in Stockholm, as part of the Graffham deception plan devised in London, a deliberate British manipulation of the Swedish Stock Exchange took place, whereby Norwegian stocks rose by almost 20 percent. This was intended to give the impression that the liberation of Norway was near, implying that Norway was one of the destinations of the Allied forces being assembled in Britain.

Not only the destination but also the imminence of the landings was hidden from the Germans. On May 9, Admiral Karl Dönitz told the Japanese ambassador in Berlin that the Allies would not be able to invade "for some time." The ambassador's radio report of this conversation, sent to Tokyo, was decrypted at Bletchley on May 13, providing welcome relief to the Anglo-American planners.

May 10 marked the first day of attacks on German long-range aircraft radar reporting stations. Between Ostend and

Cherbourg there was a German radar site every ten miles; a coastal chain of radar defenses with a parallel, but less dense, system farther inland; and many mobile radar units, guiding the German planes in their attacks. Destroying these installations was carried out by several hundred low-level attacks coordinated by Air Chief Marshal Sir Trafford Leigh-Mallory and the Typhoons and Spitfires of the Allied Expeditionary Air Force.

On May 12, United States bombers launched a massive attack on German synthetic oil plants deep inside the German Reich. The seven plants bombed that day produced together far more than a third of Germany's total output of synthetic oil, on which the German forces were now almost entirely dependent for their capacity to continue at war. Only eighty German fighters were available to meet this onslaught by eight hundred bombers.

Since the beginning of the year, the Germans had lost more than three thousand fighter pilots either killed in action or taken prisoner after their planes were shot down. Nevertheless, the German fighter pilots fought with skill and determination, shooting down forty-six bombers for the loss of thirty fighters. All seven targets were hit, three of them so seriously that they were temporarily shut down. The Germans' own Ultra messages revealed to the Allies the extent of the German alarm.

Acts of sabotage also were accelerated as the cross-Channel invasion drew nearer. On May 13, at Bagnères-de-Bigorre, in the Pyrenees, a factory producing the carriers for self-propelled guns was put out of action for six months, after an attack by British agents and French Resistance fighters. That day, along the Channel coast, Rommel inspected a new success for his planning: the completion of two formidable lines of underwater obstacles. Altogether, 517,000 obstacles had been laid down in six feet of water for high tide and half tide, 31,000 of which were fitted with mines. But two further lines of obstacles, intended for six feet of water at low tide and for twelve feet of water at low tide, were not yet in place.

On May 13, Rommel continued his tour of inspection, driving, inspecting, and conferring from division to division, throughout the area that would be attacked by the Allies if they were to land between Dieppe and Boulogne. It was a punishing, self-imposed pace, but he knew his men would be facing a determined enemy, even if he could not be certain where that enemy would strike.

In a top-secret radio signal on May 8, Rommel had warned the German High Command that the systematic Allied destruction of railways throughout northern France had begun to disrupt his supplies and troop movements. This signal was decrypted in Britain on May 14. This was a boost for the Americans as they continued their attacks. The bombing of German airfields also was proving effective, so much so that Marshal Goering ordered the Todt Organization to carry out work at airfields which were no longer used, or hardly used, to deceive the Allies into diverting bomber resources against them. Unfortunately for Goering, his order, sent by top-secret Ultra radio signal, was decrypted by British Intelligence on May 14, and the German deception was exposed.

The Germans were far more vulnerable to deception than were the Allies. On May 15 the German High Command was informed that a "good army Intelligence source" had reported the presence of units of the First United States Army Group in Yorkshire and Norfolk. The "good" source was in fact a former German agent who had long been working for Britain. The army group on which he was reporting so assiduously existed only in the minds of the Allied deception planners. Yorkshire and Norfolk were the starting points for the fictitious attacks on Norway and the Pas-de-Calais. Also on May 15 a German Military Intelligence map located a series of spurious British, American, and Norwegian military formations in Scotland. The Fortitude North deception, which set Norway as an Allied invasion objective, was working. (See the map on page 187.)

On May 12 Churchill made a tour of inspection of the troops gathering for Overlord. He began his inspection at Lydd, on the Kent coast, and ended it a hundred miles to the west, at Ascot, where Eisenhower joined him. Three days later, on May 15, he and Eisenhower were both present at a pre-D-Day briefing at St. Paul's School, Montgomery's London headquarters; King George VI also came. "As we took those uncompromisingly hard and narrow seats," wrote Rear Admiral Morton L. Deyo, who was to be the Flag Officer aboard the USS *Tuscaloosa*, "the room was hushed and the tension was palpable. . . . All in that room were aware of the gravity of the elements to be dealt with."

Eisenhower opened the proceedings with a ten-minute introduction. In Admiral Deyo's words, ". . . before the warmth of his quiet confidence the mists of doubt dissolved. When he had finished, the tension was gone. Not often has one man been called upon to accept so great a burden of responsibility. But here was one at peace with his soul."

After Eisenhower had spoken, the army plan was presented by Montgomery, the naval plan by Ramsay, and the air plan by Leigh-Mallory. Several other senior officers then spoke about their respective areas of operation. Churchill also spoke, as Major General Sir John Kennedy—Assistant Chief of the Imperial General Staff—later recalled, "for about half an hour in a robust and even humorous style, and concluded with a moving expression of his hopes and good wishes. He looked much better than when I had seen him last, and spoke with great vigour, urging offensive leadership and stressing the ardour for battle which he believed the men felt."

During his presentation Churchill used the phrase "I am hardening on the enterprise," which to those who knew of his earlier hesitations took to mean, as General Ismay wrote to Churchill, "that the more you thought about it, the more certain you were of success." Churchill explained after the war that the phrase "hardening on the enterprise" came from a telegram he had sent to General Marshall in March 1944, and that he meant the words "in the sense of wishing to strike if humanly possible, even if the limiting conditions we laid down were not exactly fulfilled."

Among those who gave briefings at the St. Paul's conference was a senior American Army Air Force officer, General Quesada. His fighter-bombers were at the cutting, destructive edge of the Transportation Plan, and they also would have a crucial role to play above the Normandy battlefield from its first hours. During Quesada's briefing, the commander of the United States VII Corps, Major General J. Lawton Collins, asked him how he was going "to keep the German Air Force from preventing our landing" on D-Day. Quesada replied: "There is not going to be any German Air Force there." Churchill, astonished by such confidence, asked Quesada how he could be so sure, to which the airman replied, "Mr. Prime Minister, because we won't let them be there. I am sure of it. There will be no German Air Force over the Normandy invasion area."

Quesada's confidence, and organizational skills, were not misplaced: on D-Day there were an astonishing ten thousand Allied planes in action. The Germans were able to put only three hundred in the air. This was not through any lack of a sense of danger; indeed, on May 18 German radio announced: "The invasion will come any day now." But Allied airpower had been used to remarkable effect. By a supreme effort of British and American fighter and bomber forces, German airpower had been all but eliminated from the imminent battlefield.

Starting on May 18, the targets of the Allied Expeditionary Air Force under Leigh-Mallory were the German radar installations used to control the German night fighters and the coastal guns of the Atlantic Wall. Within ten days, forty-two sites had been attacked and fourteen destroyed. The German ability to respond effectively to an Allied landing was being systematically weakened.

On May 20, a mere seventeen days before D-Day, the Germans still did not know where the landings would be. The German Navy was even then mining the Bay of Biscay. When Rommel asked if it could mine the Bay of the Seine—the actual Allied destination—his request was refused. He also was refused troop dispositions that could cover Normandy and Brittany at the same time, a refusal that was due, he later wrote, "to fears of a possible enemy airborne landing in the neighbourhood of Paris."

Hard evidence of the Allied destination was lacking. That same day, May 20, at his headquarters at la Roche-Guyon, Rommel personally interviewed two British officers who had been captured during one of the Tarbrush commando examinations of the beach defenses in the Pas-de-Calais. This was Tarbrush 10, which had carried out its mission on the night of May 17–18. The two men, Lieutenant Roy Woodbridge and Lieutenant George Lane, had been fired on by a German patrol. Escaping out to sea in their dinghy, they had been unable to regain the motor torpedo boat, and their dinghy drifted back to shore. There they were captured, interrogated, and then taken to Rommel.

Lieutenant Lane was offered tea by Rommel, who discussed the war with his British captive. Rommel's knowledge that Lane had been doing his work in the Pas-de-Calais area reinforced the general German conviction that the Pas-de-Calais was the invasion destination. The two officers were then sent for Gestapo interrogation and after that to a prisoner-of-war camp.

The Allied preparations moved into even higher gear. On May 21, British and American fighter-bombers launched Operation Chattanooga Choo-Choo, a systematic attack on railway engines and rolling stock throughout northern Europe, including Germany. In the first wave of attacks, almost eight hundred aircraft attacked moving trains in northern France, causing French train crews to desert in large numbers. A particularly effective method used by the fighter-bombers was to drop their external fuel tanks on the train as they flew over it the first time, then ignite the gasoline with their incendiary bullets on the return pass.

So effective were these attacks that within twenty-four hours German municipalities were urgently seeking foreign slave laborers, and even Jews from concentration camps, to help repair the bomb damage. But it could not be done.

The attacks were repeated and relentless. Eisenhower's Intelligence section had calculated that the Germans would need 175 trains a week to supply their armies once the Allied landings had been made. As a result of the fighter-bomber attacks under the Transportation Plan, that number rapidly fell to 150, and by the first week of June had tumbled to only 8—with every bridge across the Seine broken and 475 railway engines destroyed.

By mid-May more than two million American soldiers were in Britain, training and preparing for the cross-Channel landings. On May 22 the ocean liner *Mauretania,* having crossed the Atlantic from New York, docked at bomb-scarred Liverpool. Capable of carrying as many as 8,000 troops in her bunk-lined converted cabins, there were fewer than a thousand on board: the trans-Atlantic troop torrent was coming to an end. When Churchill had spotted this on his weekly Atlantic survey card, before *Mauretania* sailed, he suggested bringing home on board the ship as many British evacuee children as possible from the trans-Atlantic evacuation of the summer of 1940. Hence this author's presence—age seven—on board *Mauretania* during that mid-May voyage.

On May 23, at Sutton Coldfield, in Britain, an American officer in an Army Postal Unit who was privy to some of the D-Day secrets (such officers were known as Bigot officers) disclosed the objectives of the United States First Army to a member of the Adjutant General's department who was not a Bigot officer. The offender was sentenced to confinement for one year, with hard labor, at a United States Disciplinary Barracks, followed by dismissal from the service.

For the Allies, secrecy remained the key to the possibility of success on the day of the Normandy landings. On May 24 all camps with soldiers who were to participate in the invasion were sealed with barbed wire. Many had armed guards, to prevent unauthorized departures. That same day, senior commanders were told of the June 5 date.

Also on May 24, fewer than two weeks before the planned date for the landings, Churchill was told of a shortage of naval pumping equipment needed to raise the concrete sections of the artificial harbors. This was a last-minute and dangerous setback. He at once suggested calling on the pumping resources of the London Fire Brigade. This was done, and the crisis passed.

On May 25, British Intelligence decrypted a top-secret message from Rommel, sent six days earlier to Berlin, in which he revealed that one SS Panzer Division had no tanks and was not expecting any. It was also seriously short of officers, motor transport, and vehicle spares. Its transport included horses and bicycles. A further decrypt, of a German Air Force Enigma message, showed that the Germans expected that the landings would most probably come in the Dieppe region. The continual bombing attacks on the bridges over the Seine had led to that conclusion.

In a daylight air raid on Lyon on May 26, intended to block the German reinforcement routes from the south, railway lines, power stations, and military installations were massively bombed, but 717 French civilians were killed.

Despite a protest by the regional Resistance leader, Alban Vistel, that the local population was "painfully indignant," the Resistance efforts continued. On the day after the Lyon bombing, in an ambush set by the Resistance, twelve members of the Milice, the collaborationist Vichy French paramilitary police force, were killed. There also were many acts of sabotage. At Ambérieu, a railway engine depot was destroyed and fifty-two railway locomotives were made unusable. At Bar, in the Corrèze, a hydroelectric station was so badly damaged that it was put out of action for the next four months.

That same day, May 26, British Intelligence decrypted a message from Rommel, sent to Berlin sixteen days earlier, warning that the locomotive situation had become so serious that forced labor, and even prisoners of war, would have to be used at the repair shops; the French civilian workforce was "not responding."

Not only did the Ultra decrypts reveal to the Anglo-American planners the German Army's weaknesses and problems in France, and the strength of individual units; they also showed precisely where those units were still being sent. A series of decrypts from May 24 to May 27 showed a sudden and considerable transfer of troops—three divisions in all—to the Cotentin Peninsula. They had been directed to the very area around la Haye-du-Puits where it was intended to drop American parachute troops of the 82nd Airborne Division, the men needed to protect the landing beaches from attack from the Cotentin Peninsula. On the evening of May 27, scarcely a week before the date originally set for the landings, the Americans therefore had to abandon the plan to drop men at la Haye-du-Puits and to move the 82nd to the roadhead at Sainte-Mère-Église. The planners also had to put back the date for the capture of Cherbourg itself by seven days. Ultra had saved the Allies from the potential disaster of landing men at a point strongly held by German troops.

The deception planners also were at work that week. Operation Copperhead had been devised to create the possibility that the main Allied onslaught would not be on the Channel coast at all, but in the Mediterranean—possibly

the South of France. As it was known in Berlin that Montgomery would be heading the Allied armies—but not where—on May 26 and 27 the general appeared in Gibraltar. It was not in fact "Monty," who could not be spared from his work for such a journey, but a British officer, Lieutenant M. E. Clifton James, who was Monty's "double." Spanish agents duly reported to Berlin that the general was in Gibraltar. German Intelligence, putting the pieces at its disposal together, concluded that the Allied landing might take place in southern France, or possibly in the Balkans, one reason being that "Montgomery" had been on his way to North Africa to confer with Eisenhower's successor as Supreme Allied Commander, Mediterranean, General Sir Maitland Wilson.

The deception schemes were still working well, despite a chance cartoon in the magazine *John Bull* on May 27 in which the plump British soldier "Old Bill," a strategic know-it-all, while talking to an American soldier next to a cow whose markings are the map of Europe, puts his fingers exactly on Normandy and says, "If yer asks me, mate, that's where Eisenhower gone to land, right there!" Perhaps German Intelligence thought it was a subtle British deception effort to divert their attention from the Pas-de-Calais.

On May 28, American bombers made their second raid on five of the German synthetic oil plants, which they had already damaged on May 12. That night, British bombers attacked the reinforced concrete fortifications at St-Martin-de-Varreville, overlooking the Utah invasion beach; a block-house, command posts and signals equipment were destroyed. The air bombardment of railway marshaling yards also had continued, resulting not only in the disruption of German military movements by rail but also in a total of three thousand French civilian deaths in forty-eight hours. "Terrible things are being done," Churchill wrote to British Foreign Secretary Anthony Eden on May 28. On the following day, after reading the reports of the attacks during May 28, Churchill wrote again, to Air Chief Marshal Tedder, the Deputy Supreme Commander of the Allied Expeditionary Forces: "You are piling up an awful load of hatred."

Hatred or not, the bombing was effective. On May 28 the destruction of the German naval radio station at Château Terlinden, near Bruges, made it much more difficult for German Intelligence to "hear" the extra volume of Allied radio traffic that would indicate the imminence of an Anglo-American land, air, and sea assault.

The German Air Force, once so boastful under Goering, and capable of sustained and devastating bomber attacks, no longer had the resources both to bomb Britain and to prepare for the inevitable air battles of a cross-Channel attack. For their part, the Allies were carrying out Operation Crossbow, attacking the flying bomb "Ski" sites from the Pas-de-Calais to Dieppe. By the end of May these sites were protected by 520 heavy guns and a further 730 guns of lighter caliber. In these Crossbow attacks 154 Allied aircraft had been shot down by the end of May, with 771 aircrew dead or missing. But as many as two-thirds of the "Ski" sites from which the flying bomb would be launched had been put out of action.

·   ·   ·

On May 29 German Air Force Intelligence reversed its earlier assessment that the Allied landing would come between Le Havre and Cherbourg. The landing might be as far to the east as Dieppe, the Intelligence experts concluded. This was a triumph for Allied deception plans and a remarkable bonus for the Allies, who decrypted this signal on the day it was sent.

That same day, the order went out that all Allied vehicles that were to participate in the landings be painted on their sides and top with a white star in a white circle, "to facilitate recognition both from the air and by the land troops." All Allied aircraft were to have three broad white stripes painted on their wings. All over Britain, the painting was begun, the vehicles all being painted before they moved to their marshaling areas near the South Coast. French money—from the year 1938—was issued to all troops, together with a specially written handbook, *France*. Then the men and armor began to move to their final staging areas.

Rommel continued to inspect his beach defenses in Normandy, as elsewhere along the coast. On May 30 he watched a demonstration of weaponry by the 21st SS Panzer Division at Lion-sur-Mer, a small seaside town that was on the western flank of the imminent Sword Beach landing area. Four pieces of equipment were demonstrated, firing out to sea: a rocket launcher and three types of multi-barreled grenade launchers. There was to be no letup in the attempt to ensure that any Allied landings would be repulsed, but Allied airpower had become a strong weapon against Rommel's preparations. On May 31 an Allied air raid over northern France cut the German Air Force overland telephone cable at a point between Paris and Rouen and interrupted telephonic communication between German headquarters in Paris and German Air Force bases around both Rennes and Caen for three crucial days.

The Allied deception schemes on which so much depended had all worked. As the Normandy landings drew near, it was known by British Intelligence that more than 372,000 German troops were tied down in Norway, held there in anticipation of an Anglo-Soviet amphibious attempt.

D-Day had been fixed for June 5, but the actual timing of the assault, H-Hour, was still not decided on. The decision was made on May 28. The landings would be in two waves, the first "a few minutes before 0600 hours" and the second "after 0700 hours." To allow for differences in the time of low tide, the Americans would land at Utah and Omaha first, followed a few minutes later by the British on Gold and Sword and the Canadians on Juno.

On the day this decision was made Eisenhower moved elements of his headquarters from Bushey to Southwick House near Portsmouth, near to where Montgomery had moved a month earlier, although Eisenhower still spent part of the day at Bushey. Both men wanted to be near the embarkation ports during the days of the most intense activity, expectation, and final preparation. On May 31 the first troops and men were loaded on board ship at Portsmouth and Southampton. That night, three Harbor Defense Motor Launches (HDMLs) crossed the Channel, laying a total of 830 buoys at the northern ends of the ten approach channels that were to be swept by minesweepers across the known German minefields. The buoys were primed to transmit a radio signal to all Allied landing craft on six successive days, starting on June 4.

8

The First Five Days
of June

On June 1, the second day on which the Allied troops and vehicles in Britain were being loaded on board ship, the Anglo-American planners of the Normandy landings, set for June 5, were shown the decrypt of a telegram from the Japanese Ambassador in Berlin, Count Oshima, to Tokyo.

In his telegram, Oshima reported on a conversation that he had had with Hitler four days earlier, when Hitler told Oshima that the Allies had completed their preparations; that they had assembled eighty divisions, eight of which had combat experience and were "very good troops"; that after diversionary operations in Norway, Denmark, southwestern France, and on the French Mediterranean coast, they would establish a bridgehead in Normandy or Brittany; and that after seeing how things went, they would embark on establishing a real second front in the Dover Strait.

Several things were clear from Hitler's conversation: while the Germans regarded an invasion either in Normandy or Brittany as definite, they did not know which it would be,

nor did they regard it as imminent; several diversionary operations elsewhere were expected to come first. Also, it was
believed in Berlin that the Pas-de-Calais would be the true
focus of the main assault on Fortress Europe.

June 1 held a moment of concern for the Allied
Intelligence services. That morning, the London *Daily
Telegraph* crossword puzzle included the clue "Britannia and
he hold the same thing," the answer to which was
Neptune—the code name for the Allied naval assault.* A
scrutiny of the paper's crossword puzzles over the previous
month revealed four other D-Day code words. Two of them
were the American landing beaches: "One of the US" on
May 2 (Utah), and "Red Indian on the Missouri" on May
22 (Omaha).† On May 27 came the code word for the
whole operation: "but some bigwig has stolen some of it at
times" (Overlord).‡ And on May 30 the artificial harbors:
"This bush is a centre of nursery revolutions" (Mulberry).§

The man who had devised these crossword puzzles,
Leonard Dawe, was the headmaster of a school in southern
England. Questioned by Military Intelligence, it emerged
that his choice of these particular clues had been entirely
fortuitous, although his brother-in-law did work at the
Admiralty. He had, he said, compiled those particular crossword puzzles some months earlier. Fortunately, the clues
were not noticed by German Intelligence or matched up
with anything they might have gleaned elsewhere. Their

---

*Because both Britannia and Neptune hold a trident.
† Utah was one of the United States; Omahas were an Indian tribe on the
Missouri River.
‡ I have been unable to find anyone who can explain how this clue leads to
Overlord.
§ "Here we go round the mulberry bush."

own spies in Britain had long ago been captured and shot—or, like Garbo, were working steadily against them.

For the Allied planners, June 1 marked the first day of an intense pattern of consultations. Each morning and evening all the senior commanders met at Southwick House, Portsmouth, to discuss the final details of the imminent invasion. General Montgomery and Admiral Ramsay were already at Portsmouth. Eisenhower continued to make daily shuttles there by car from his headquarters at Bushey, traveling via his Air Headquarters at Stanmore. The main concern at the twice-daily meetings in Portsmouth was the deteriorating condition of the weather. The tides, which were immutable, determined that June 5, 6, or 7 were the only realistic days that month; it was the weather that was flexible and unpredictable.

Bad weather seemed to make a postponement inevitable. In a most secret radio signal to Berlin, Field Marshal von Rundstedt had stated that the Allies would need four consecutive days of good weather to carry out a cross-Channel assault. No such four-day-clear period was forecast. He, Rundstedt, was therefore certain that the invasion could not take place in the first week of June.

The secret communications code that von Rundstedt had used for his message about the weather was in a cypher the British had broken. His message was therefore decrypted at Bletchley and passed on immediately to Eisenhower. From that moment, as a result of reading not only the message but also the mind of his opposite number, Eisenhower knew that if he could launch the invasion in conditions ruled out by von Rundstedt, he would catch the Germans unaware.

In Britain, amid tight security, the Allied troops were beginning to board ship at more than twenty-two ports. (See the map on page 194.) The Canadian 3rd Division—comprising fifteen thousand Canadian and nine thousand British troops—began to board at Southampton on June 1. That night, among the frequent BBC messages broadcast to Resistance circuits in France was one that consisted of the first three lines of a poem by Paul Verlaine. The lines were: *Les sanglots longs/des violons/de l'automne* (The long sobs of the violins of autumn). The Germans wrongly believed that these lines were addressed to all Resistance circuits in France, and that when the next three lines were broadcast it would mean that invasion would follow within forty-eight hours. In fact, the lines were directed to a single Resistance circuit, Ventriloquist, working south of Orléans, instructing it to stand by for the next three lines, which would be the signal for it to carry out its railway-cutting tasks—in conjunction with the Allied landings.

Because of the distance to be covered, the first warships that would be bombarding the German positions on the landing beaches set sail from the Clyde on June 2. This was Bombardment Force D; its destination, Sword Beach. In the air war, the final, devastating preliminaries were reaching their conclusion. On the night of June 2, British bombers again bombed the French railway marshaling yards at Trappes. This raid marked the culmination of the Transportation Plan, which had begun on March 6. Within three months, more than eight thousand British bombers had dropped 42,000 tons of bombs on railway marshaling yards in France and Belgium.

Also on June 2 the Allied Expeditionary Air Force began a series of low-level attacks on the twelve most important remaining German radar sites along the Channel coast. Six were chosen as targets by the navy, six by the air force. In the attack on June 2 made by eighteen Typhoons against the radar site at Caudecote, near Dieppe, considerable damage was done, for the loss of one Typhoon. But the radar sites were well defended, and in attacks on other sites the Allied losses were higher. But the German radar capacity—on the eve of battle—was gravely weakened.

The weather over the Channel, bad on June 2, began to deteriorate in the early afternoon of June 3. The German forecasters predicted bad weather for the next three or four days. This ruled out June 5 or June 6 as days on which an assault would be launched.

Had German Intelligence been aware of the increased Allied radio traffic, they might have reviewed this confident assumption. But on the night of June 3–4 they suffered a severe, decisive setback. That night the German radio intercept station on the Cotentin Peninsula, at Urville-Hague—the headquarters of the German Signals Intelligence service in northwestern France—was completely destroyed ("wiped off the map" in the words of Leigh-Mallory) by air attack. The site had been identified by British Signals Intelligence decrypters at Bletchley. After the landings Leigh-Mallory called its destruction "an important contributory factor to the lack of enemy air reaction to the assault."

Rommel had visited von Rundstedt on June 3, at his headquarters at St-Germain-en-Laye, just outside Paris, to talk about Rommel's proposed visit to Germany. He would start, he said, on June 5, and return four days later. The visit had a twofold purpose. Rommel would be at home with his wife on her birthday, and he would then go to see Hitler, both to impress on him "the extent of the manpower and material inferiority we would suffer in the event of a landing," and to request the dispatch to northern France of two further Panzer divisions, an anti-aircraft corps, and other reinforcements.

Von Rundstedt saw no problem in Rommel's departure. He knew that the weather was such that the Allies would not attack during that period and that they would have to delay until at least the end of the month. Eisenhower also knew that the bad weather made it impossible to go ahead on June 5. At four-fifteen that morning he postponed the invasion for twenty-four hours. Both the juxtaposition of the moon positions and the tide, plus the precious knowledge that the Germans expected no assault anywhere for the next three to four days, made it desirable that too great a delay beyond June 5 should be avoided.

During the morning of June 4 all the Allied convoys already crossing the Channel were ordered back to their ports. But the two Royal Navy midget submarines, *X20* and *X23*, which would have to act as markers for the invasion forces, were instructed to continue on their way, to the extremity of the landing zone. That morning of June 4 there was a forecast of a brief spell of better weather. But it was less than the four clear days that the Germans regarded as the Allied minimum; it was therefore unlikely that the Germans would be alerted or alarmed. Thanks to knowledge provided by Ultra, the risks to the Allies of launching the invasion under the poor prevailing weather conditions would be more than compensated for.

At six on the morning of June 4, Rommel—in the blustery rain and wind, which, by his calculations, ruled out an Allied invasion for at least two weeks and possibly three—

left his headquarters at la Roche-Guyon for the long drive to Germany. In Britain, Montgomery was driven to Tarrant Rushton, where the men involved in a crucial predawn aspect of the landings were ready for their mission.

Tarrant Rushton was where the last training exercises had taken place for the airborne capture of two bridges, one over the Orne Canal and the other, three hundred yards to the east, over the River Orne. The glider pilots had been trained at Tarrant Rushton by Derek "Tommy" Grant, a pilot and glider expert who, in the words of his obituary in *The Times* of London in the year 2002, "flew with each glider crew in turn, coaching, encouraging and analysing each exercise and every minor mishap, so as to ensure the required precision."

The capture of the two Orne bridges was an essential preliminary to securing the eastern flank of the landing. The assault was to be carried out by D Company of the glider-borne Ox and Bucks Light Infantry, commanded by Major John Howard. Sixteen pilots would land the gliders by moonlight, soon after midnight. About thirty men would travel in each glider. Montgomery wanted to see the gliders that would be used and to talk to Howard about the attack. He was satisfied with what he saw and heard.

There had been one cause for particular concern. As Howard and his men had studied the aerial photographs taken almost daily by low-flying Royal Air Force planes, they saw a steady increase in the number of poles—"Rommel's asparagus"—that were being erected in the fields around the bridges—wherever the defenders felt, correctly, that gliders might land. But when Howard confided his concern to Jim Wallwork, the pilot of his glider, Wallwork was pleased. The poles, he said, would help the gliders to stop.

For the troops landing from the sea, Rommel had devised a far more formidable obstacle, a minefield strip one thousand mines deep along the whole Channel coast, with an astonishing density of ten mines per square meter. Fortunately for the men about to land, of the planned 20 million mines that would have constituted this obstacle, only 3 million had been laid by D-Day. It was nevertheless a danger, albeit one to which the Allies were alerted.

June 4 was the fourth anniversary of the final day of the Dunkirk evacuation in 1940. That day, Admiral Ramsay—who had supervised the naval aspects of that evacuation and was now in charge of Neptune—went down to some of the "hards" to watch the loading of the tank landing craft. He was upset to see that they were being overloaded, which, he later wrote, "was the fault of the Army, whose one idea was to cram as many vehicles and as much into each vehicle as possible."

Also on June 4 Churchill and Eisenhower met General Charles de Gaulle near Eisenhower's headquarters on the South Coast. Immediately after Dunkirk, de Gaulle had set up the Free French Movement in Britain, and in 1943 he had established the French Committee of National Liberation in Algiers. Churchill and Roosevelt had declined to regard de Gaulle's committee as the sole representative of France; indeed, Roosevelt wanted, once Allied forces were in France, to set up an Allied military administration there. Only then would he allow Eisenhower to consult with de Gaulle about the political future of the country.

De Gaulle and his committee had not been told of the D-Day landings or the Overlord plan. Even General Pierre

Koenig, whose clandestine Free French Forces of the Interior (FFI) were based in London, was not let in to the secret. Yet his men and women inside France were already active in disrupting German communications, and would have to do so on D-Day itself, and after D-Day.

As a gesture of defiance to the Anglo-American position, on May 26 the French Committee of National Liberation had proclaimed itself the Provisional Government of the French Republic. Churchill and Roosevelt were furious. At the meeting with Churchill and Eisenhower on June 4, de Gaulle was told of the imminent landings, but he had strong grievances that he put to them with vigor. First, he refused to accept the Allied plan to introduce its own currency into France. When Churchill suggested that he refer the matter to Roosevelt, de Gaulle was furious. "Why do you think that I need to submit my candidacy for the authority in France to Roosevelt?" he asked. Then he was told by Eisenhower that he, Eisenhower, would broadcast a proclamation to the French people. Eisenhower invited him to do likewise. Again de Gaulle was furious, asking the Supreme Commander: "You broadcast a proclamation to the French people? And by what right? And what will you tell them?" Permitted to broadcast to France, de Gaulle told his listeners, "The directions issued by the French government and the French leaders who have been delegated to issue them must be followed to the letter."

At nine o'clock on the evening of June 4 a crucial meeting took place at Eisenhower's headquarters. Those present had to decide whether to launch the cross-Channel landing then, or to postpone it, because of the uncertain weather, perhaps for several weeks. One of those present, Air Vice

Marshal James Robb, kept a note of the discussion. It began with Admiral Ramsay stressing that the first orders to the naval forces—those to the Western Task Force, which would be in action first—would have to go out "within the next half hour" if the landings were to take place on the morning of June 6.

Eisenhower believed that the weather conditions for June 6 were "almost ideal up to a point"—that was the best that the weather experts could forecast. When Leigh-Mallory said that, weatherwise, the early hours of June 5 would not be a good time for his bombers, as Bomber Command would have "great difficulty" in getting their markers down, several of those present at the meeting pointed out to him that he was talking about the wrong night—his bombers would not be required to carry out their pre-D-Day attacks on the German shore fortifications until the early hours of June 6. Eisenhower also told Leigh-Mallory: "Don't be that pessimistic."

Eisenhower then asked Montgomery if he saw any reason "for not going" on June 6. Montgomery replied, "I would say—Go!" Eisenhower agreed. The alternatives were, he said, "too chancy"; the question was "just how long can you hang this operation on the end of a limb and let it hang there." When Leigh-Mallory again raised his fears of the situation in the air, warning that there would be a "hell of a situation" if the German night bombers were able to operate and the Allied night fighters could not, and mentioning Dieppe, Eisenhower cut him off (at the word "Dieppe") and pointed out that if Leigh-Mallory did not give the instructions to his airmen at once, he would be unable to give them on the night of the sixth; it would be too late.

Then Eisenhower cast the die, telling the land, sea, and air commanders: "Well, I'm quite positive we must give the order; the only question is whether we should meet again in the morning." This was agreed. Then Eisenhower said, "Well, I don't like it, but there it is." And finally, "Well, boys, there it is, I don't see how we can possibly do anything else."

These words were hardly the "Okay, we'll go," "Okay, let's go," or "Okay, let 'er rip" more terse utterances, with each one of which Eisenhower was later credited; but his actual words were decisive enough. The operation would be launched on June 6. The orders would go out at once, and throughout the night of June 4–5, so that from the early hours of June 5 every part of the complex, interwoven, intricate mechanism of an amphibious landing would be on the move.

The decision to avoid a further day's—or more—postponement averted the danger that, despite the incredible success thus far of the Allied deception schemes, the Germans might discover what was afoot. It was also the case that, with so many soldiers already at sea, "any more delay" (in the words of Major and Mrs. Holt) "and the seasick army might not be fit to fight."

On the evening of June 5, American troops reached the center of Rome, the first capital city to be liberated by the Western Allies. At eleven o'clock that night, two Royal Navy midget submarines, *X20* and *X23*, were in place off the Normandy coast, to mark the western edge of the British landing beaches—when the moment came for them to do so.

On the morning of June 5, Eisenhower wrote a message, in his own hand, to be published in the event of failure. It read: "Our landings in the Cherbourg-Havre area have failed to gain a satisfactory foothold and I have withdrawn the troops. My decision to attack at this time and place was based upon the best information available. The troops, the air, and the Navy did all that bravery and devotion to duty could do. If any blame or fault attaches to the attempt it is mine alone."

The meeting at Eisenhower's headquarters at four-fifteen that morning was, Air Vice Marshal Robb noted, "very brief." The overnight weather charts were examined, and nothing was found to alter the previous evening's decision to go. The orders had already gone out to start the day's military, air, and naval moves.

During June 5 a message from Montgomery was read to all troops preparing to embark for Normandy. Their Commander-in-Chief had his own distinctive style, and also a quotation from the seventeenth-century soldier-poet the Earl of Montrose. "Monty's" message read:

1. The time has come to deal the enemy a terrific blow in Western Europe.

   The blow will be struck by the combined sea, land, and air forces of the Allies—together constituting one great Allied team, under the supreme command of General Eisenhower.

2. On the eve of this great adventure I send my best wishes to every soldier in the Allied team.

   To us is given the honour of striking a blow for freedom which will live in history; and in the better days that lie ahead men will speak with pride of our doings. We have a great and a righteous cause.

   Let us pray that "The Lord Mighty in Battle" will go forth with our armies, and that His special providence will aid us in the struggle.

3. I want every soldier to know that I have complete confidence in the successful outcome of the operations that we are now about to begin.

   With stout hearts, and with enthusiasm for the contest, let us go forward to victory.

4. And, as we enter the battle, let us recall the words of a famous soldier spoken many years ago:

> He either fears his fate too much,
>   Or his deserts are small,
> Who dare not put it to the touch,
>   To win or lose it all.

5. Good luck to each one of you. And good hunting on the mainland of Europe.

On the afternoon of June 5 the German Army Intelligence Service informed General Jodl that during the previous night the two lines of poetry from a poem by Paul Verlaine had been heard by the Security Section of the Fifteenth Army. These were the two lines that had been given as the warning order to one of the Resistance circuits about imminent invasion, to be followed by the more immediate warning of forty-eight hours' notice.

Jodl and his advisers took no action. The lines gave no clue as to their meaning. However, the Commander-in-Chief of the Fifteenth Army, Colonel General Hans von Salmuth, sensed that something was afoot and ordered standby on the evening of June 5. But even he waited to give the order until shortly before midnight, after he had received "numerous reports of major sea and air movements" from his Intelligence service.

It must therefore be presumed, commented General

Walter Warlimont, who was serving in Hitler's headquarters at the time, "that none of those involved, including Jodl, attached much importance to the information." Alternatively, he wrote, "they may have been waiting for some more definite confirmation."

At five o'clock on the afternoon of June 5 the tens of thousands of Allied soldiers on board their ships were addressed by Tannoy loudspeaker systems. The message was brief and unambiguous. For the troops of the Green Howards, who were to land at Gold Beach, and who had been on board *Empire Lance,* at anchor off the Solent, for the past five days, its clarity was a relief: "At 1745 hours this ship will weigh anchor and, in passage with the remainder of the armada, sail for the coast of France." Waiting was over. Seasickness would soon come to an end. The battle for which they had trained so long was about to begin.

Also that afternoon the First United States Army Commander, General Bradley, sailed for the beachhead on board Admiral Ernest King's flagship *Augusta.* Shortly after Bradley had sailed, Ultra revealed that a crack German unit, the 352nd Infantry Brigade, had moved to the area of Omaha Beach. Since strict radio silence had been imposed throughout the fleet for the period of the cross-Channel movement, there was no way by which Bradley could warn the assault troops. "And before it was cut to pieces," General Walter Bedell Smith later wrote, "the 352nd gave all too good an account of itself against the American 1st and 29th Divisions the following day."

That evening Eisenhower drove from his headquarters in Portsmouth to Newbury, to visit the airfields in the area from which American airborne troops would be taking off just before midnight. (See the map on page 192.) His driver, Kay Summersby, later recalled how, after a day in which "the pace was unrelenting," at six that evening "we dropped everything to make the long drive to Newbury and visit the 101st Airborne. They would be the first troops to land in Normandy behind the enemy lines. Some would be towed over in huge gliders that would settle down quietly in the darkness with their cargoes of young fighting men. Others would parachute down into this heavily fortified area. Ike's last task on the eve of D-Day was to wish these men well."

There was "no military pomp" about Eisenhower's visit, Kay Summersby recalled. "His flag was not flying from the radiator of the car, and he had told me to cover the four stars on the red plate. We drove up to each of the airfields, and Ike got out and just started walking among the men. When they realized who it was, the word went from group to group like the wind blowing across a meadow, and then everyone went crazy. The roar was unbelievable. They cheered and whistled and shouted, 'Good old Ike!' There they were, these young paratroopers in their bulky combat kits with their faces blackened so that they would be invisible in the dark of the French midnight. Anything that could not be carried in their pockets was strapped on their backs or to their arms and legs. Many of them had packages of cigarettes strapped to their thighs.

"They looked so young and so brave," Kay Summersby continued. "I stood by the car and watched as the General walked among them with his military aide a few paces behind him. He went from group to group and shook hands with as many men as he could. He spoke a few words to every man as he shook his hand, and he looked the man in the eye as he wished him success." Eisenhower later told Kay

Summersby: "It's very hard really to look a soldier in the eye when you fear that you are sending him to his death."

The first airfield of the 101st Airborne that Eisenhower visited was at Greenham Common. One of the paratroopers there, Wallace Strobell, recalled how Eisenhower asked him his name and which State he came from. "I gave him my name and I said I was from Michigan. 'Oh, yes, Michigan . . . great fishing there . . . been there several times and like it.' He then asked if I felt we were ready for the operation, did I feel we had been well briefed and were all ready for the drop. I replied we were all set and didn't think we would have too much of a problem." Strobell added: "He seemed in good spirits. He chatted a little more, which I believe was intended to relax us, and I think that all of us being keyed up and ready to go buoyed him up somewhat."

From Greenham Common, Eisenhower went to Aldermaston, then to Welford, and finally to Membury. Time was running out, so he did not go on to the fifth air-field, at Ramsbury. Instead, he returned to Greenham Common to watch the takeoff. Then he returned to Portsmouth, telling Kay Summersby during the drive back, "I hope to God I know what I am doing."

At nine that evening, at Spithead, Piper Bill Millin piped off No. 6 Commando, at the start of their all-night cross-Channel journey to Sword Beach. Thirty minutes later, the second three lines of the Verlaine poem—*blessent mon coeur/d'une langueur/monotone* (pierce my heart with a monotonous dullness)—were broadcast over the BBC to the Ventriloquist Resistance circuit, instructing it to act at once in carrying out its railway-cutting sabotage. The SS Security Service radio interception section in Paris heard this as it was broadcast. Believing, rightly, that the broadcast of the second section of the poem was related to invasion, but wrongly, that it was an Allied call for railway sabotage throughout France, the Security Service immediately alerted the German High Command in the West. An hour later, the German Fifteenth Army warned its various corps that intercepted messages pointed to an invasion within forty-eight hours (the parachute landings were fewer than three hours away). The German force responsible for most of the imminent assault area, the Seventh Army, which had received too many false warnings in the past, took no action.

At ten minutes past eleven that night, the seven hundred British paratroopers of the 9th Parachute Battalion (9 Para) took off in Dakotas from RAF Harwell for the airborne assault on the Merville Battery.

The bad weather on June 5 kept almost all the German Air Force reconnaissance aircraft grounded. Five reconnaissance sorties were flown, but none reported any unusual activity in the ports of southern England. At nine-thirty that evening a coded British radio message, sent openly on the BBC, instructed French Resistance operatives to cut railway lines throughout France. German Intelligence, which had partially broken the code, warned Rommel's headquarters at la Roche-Guyon; but in Rommel's absence no notice seems to have been taken of the warning. Of 1,050 breaches of the railway lines planned between their British contacts and the French Resistance circuits, and activated by a series of "innocent" messages, 950 were carried out, an amazing and effective achievement.

The "Pimento" circuit halted all German rail traffic between Toulouse and Montauban. The "Jockey" circuit ensured that every train leaving Marseille for Lyon after

D-Day was derailed at least once in its journey. The "Farmer" circuit ensured that the railway junctions around Lille and Tourcoing were cut within two nights of D-Day and kept cut until the end of the month.

On the evening of June 5, at air bases throughout Britain, the final painting was being done to ensure that there were white stripes on the wings and fuselages of every aircraft about to set off for France. Irving Rosenbluth, a clerk in the supply office of one of the bases, recalled: "Everyone on the base who was not part of a flight crew was given a can of paint, a brush, and assigned a plane. We got the job done, but I was never sure the paint on the plane was dry by the time they took off. Some of the men argued that there was more paint on us than on the plane. . . ." Flight crews were given instructions to shoot down any plane they saw that did not have the white stripes.

At eight o'clock that evening there began what Admiral Ramsay called "the largest single minesweeping operation that had yet been undertaken in war." Ten approach channels for the assault forces—the entrances to which had already been marked with radio-transmitting buoys—were carved out through the German minefields. Despite stronger tidal flows than had been allowed for, all went according to plan. Even when the minesweepers were in sight of the German coast, no German batteries fired on them. It was dark, the weather was stormy, and they completed their task uninterrupted.

Last-minute efforts were made to confirm that the beaches could sustain the weight of armor that was about to be put on them. General Bradley later recalled how, on the day after the landings, he received an urgent inquiry as to whether the subsoil on Omaha Beach really was suitable for any further heavy equipment—desperately needed by the men who would be pinned down there, pounded by German artillery. Was it treacherous silt? He asked Bradley. The reply was brought to him, he wrote, by "a lean and reticent British naval lieutenant," who pulled out of his pocket a thick glass tube and proceeded to explain that, on the night of June 5–6, he had been taken by submarine through the as yet uncleared minefields off the coast of Normandy, had paddled ashore in a rubber boat—unseen by the German gunners in their concrete casemates—and had drilled a core in the shingle at a point designated on the map. "You can see by this core," the lieutenant told Bradley, holding up the tube, "there is no evidence of silt. The shingle is firmly bedded upon the rock. There is little danger of your trucks bogging down."

No such confidence was present among the German planners. A message sent by the German Air Force High Command late on June 5 showed how short the Germans were of aviation fuel. The message was an instruction to the First Parachute Army, based at Nancy, to conserve consumption of aircraft fuel. "With reduction of aircraft fuel by Allied action," the message read, "most essential requirements for training and carrying out production plans can scarcely be covered by quantities of aircraft fuel available." Wherever possible, the supply of goods to air units, and "duty journeys in general," must be made by rail. Decrypted at Bletchley, this boosted the confidence of the Allied air force commanders, even as their planes were flying toward France.

The greatest amphibious landing yet attempted was about to begin. "Tonight we go," Churchill telegraphed to Stalin.

"We are using five thousand ships and have available eleven thousand aircraft." And to Clementine, his wife, Churchill confided his deepest fears, telling her, "Do you realize that by the time you wake up in the morning, twenty thousand men may have been killed?" The Allied Expeditionary Forces were about to be pitted against a Germany that was master of Europe from the Arctic Ocean to the Aegean Sea, and from the Bay of Biscay to the Black Sea. (See the map on page 193.)

John Keegan, at that time a ten-year-old schoolboy living on the outskirts of Taunton, in the West Country, who was later to write extensively about the Normandy landings, recalled an incident that night witnessed by so many Britons: ". . . the sky over our house began to fill with the sound of aircraft, which swelled until it overflowed the darkness from edge to edge. Its first tremors had taken my parents into the garden, and as the roar grew I followed and stood between them to gaze awestruck at the constellation of red, green and yellow lights, which rode across the heavens and streamed southward towards the sea. It seemed as if every aircraft in the world was in flight, as wave followed wave without intermission, dimly discernible as darker corpuscles on the black plasma of the clouds, which the moon had not yet risen to illuminate. The element of noise in which they swam became solid, blocking our ears, entering our lungs and beating the ground beneath our feet with the relentless surge of an ocean swell. Long after the last had passed from view and the thunder of their passage had died into the silence of the night, restoring to our consciousness the familiar and timeless elements of our surroundings, elms, hedges, rooftops, clouds and stars, we remained transfixed and wordless on the spot where we stood, gripped by a wild surmise of what the power, majesty and menace of the great migratory flight could portend."

Shortly before midnight, six British infantrymen of the 6th Airborne Division posed for a photographer next to their glider. On it they had chalked their defiant messages. The main one read: "The Channel Stopped You, But Not Us." Another declared: "Remember Coventry, Plymouth, Bristol, London. Now It's Our Turn."

9

D-Day

From Midnight to Dawn

Five minutes before midnight on June 5, British infantrymen, members of the 6th Airborne Division, landed by gliders at the village of Bénouville, six miles north of Caen. Operation Overlord had begun. By dawn, 18,000 British, American, and Canadian parachutists were on the ground behind Utah and Sword Beaches, capturing bridges and strong points and disrupting German lines of communication.

During the night of June 5–6 the first three thousand of more than seven thousand Allied warships—British, American, Canadian, Polish, Dutch, Norwegian, French, and Greek, the combined forces of Operation Neptune—were crossing the Channel, bringing the first of more than 150,000 men who were to land during the day. As this vast armada drew ever closer to the Normandy beaches, a new series of deceptions was launched to draw German attention to other possible destinations. One deception, using motor launches and radio signals to simulate the movement of a large convoy, was a spurious cross-Channel assault toward the beaches between Le Havre and Dieppe. A second, designed to suggest a similar amphibious threat east of Le Havre, was carried out by motor launches off Harfleur. A third deception, Operation Glimmer, took the form of a substantial air attack on the fortifications in the Pas-de-Calais.

A fourth deception that night, the largest of the four, Operation Taxable, was twofold: the dropping of dummy parachutists near Boulogne, together with the dropping over the Channel of tens of thousands of radar-jamming metallic strips, known as Window. These strips were dropped in such a way as to produce on German radar screens the appearance of a large, slow-moving convoy making its way across the Channel toward the Pas-de-Calais. The Window drop was carried out by Group Captain Leonard Cheshire's 617 Squadron. The operation had to be timed to perfection so that the clouds of metal strips, dropped at precise intervals by successive waves of aircraft, gave the impression to the German radar watchers of the steady approach of shipping at a speed of nine knots. "Any aberration," explained Cheshire's 1992 obituary in *The Times* of London, "would have given the game away."

Underneath the clouds of Window as it fell were Royal Navy motor gunboats—in Operation Moonshine—carrying special electronic equipment that could respond to German radar signals by amplifying and repeating their pulse, so that a single gunboat showed all the symptoms of many large ships. Experimented with since 1942, Moonshine was the first use of this radar deception in a large-scale amphibious landing. It was yet another component of the vast, intricate assemblage that made up the D-Day plan.

The Pas-de-Calais deception worked. The phantom armada was clearly visible on German radar, diverting the attention of the German coastal and fighter defenses away from the real invasion force that was even then heading toward the beaches of Normandy, 150 miles to the south-west. Indeed, as the bogus convoy came within range of the massive German 12-inch gun batteries in the Pas-de-Calais, those guns fired salvo after salvo at the clouds of descending tinsel. In broadcasting the first German account of the Normandy landings on the following day, Dr. Joseph Goebbels, Hitler's Propaganda Minister, added that there were "landing troops" outside Calais and Dunkirk.

In the early hours of June 6, two groups of parachutists, a dozen in each group, dropped near the town of Isigny, ten miles southeast of Omaha Beach. It was the ultimate deception operation, ordered by the ever-inventive Colonel Bevan and the London Controlling Section. Code-named Titanic, its aim was to distract the Germans by pretending that it constituted a major parachute landing. One of its planners was Captain M. R. D. Foot, who had earlier been involved in choosing areas in France where German reinforcements to Normandy could most effectively be harried by the French Resistance under SOE guidance (Foot was later to be the historian of SOE in France).

Two groups of parachutists, each of five men, members of the Special Air Service Brigade, took part in Titanic. On landing on French soil they fired Very lights to illuminate the bogus dropping zone and played recordings on gramophone records of small-arms fire interspersed with soldiers' conversation. In addition to the real drop, a thousand dummy parachutists were dropped, to give the impression of a major landing.

As its planners in Whitehall intended, Operation Titanic deceived the Germans. At three in the morning, which was 3½ hours before the Omaha Beach landings, the German 915th Infantry Regiment (the reserve brigade of the division holding the sector) was sent eastward to "counter an airborne threat" near Isigny and spent the whole morning—while the Americans who had landed at Omaha were at their most vulnerable—searching for the spurious Titanic parachutists in the woods around Isigny and even exchanging fire with them. By the time the German regiment was sent to Omaha, where fighting had been particularly severe, the American troops there had finally managed to secure the beachhead. "In the regiment," writes M. R. D. Foot, "Titanic is remembered as a disaster, for a sound regimental reason—of the ten men who went on it, only two came back." But it was a masterpiece of successful deception. Without it, the Americans on Omaha might have been thrown back into the sea.

As the "real" parachutists at Utah and Sword worked in darkness on what had been enemy-occupied soil for the previous four years, a thousand aircraft of Royal Air Force Bomber Command began a sustained attack on the main German coastal batteries in the area soon to be assaulted from the sea.* Two of the bomber squadrons were in action for the first time—consisting of Free French pilots and aircrew—the Groupe Guyenne and the Groupe Tunisie, that

---

* These batteries were at Crisbecq, St-Martin-de-Varreville, Ouistreham, Maisy, Mont Fleury, Pointe du Hoc, Merville-Franceville, Houlgate, and Longues. (See the maps on pages 196 and 197.)

were attached to a British bomber group. Their specific target was the fortified German gun emplacements outside Grand-camp-Maisy, with their clear line of fire on what within a few hours was to be Utah Beach.

As the planes of RAF Bomber Command left the assault area, more than a thousand United States bombers of the Eighth Air Force took over, and, in the thirty minutes before the troops were to land, they dropped 2,796 tons of bombs on the same coastal defenses. That morning, above the Irish Sea and the Bay of Biscay, a Czechoslovak air squadron took part in Operation Cork, a twenty-one-squadron operation to intercept and destroy all German submarines making their way to the Channel to interrupt the Allied armada. Ultra decrypts gave the British a clear picture of the movement of all thirty-six U-boats that had been ordered from their bases on the Atlantic coast of France to the Channel. Seventeen left from Brest, fourteen from St-Nazaire, four from La Pallice, and one from Lorient. All but nine of them, not fitted with a Schnorchel apparatus, had to surface regularly to recharge their batteries and top up their high-pressure air. That made them exceedingly vulnerable to air attack.

A Canadian pilot, a volunteer from Vancouver, Flying Officer Kenneth O. Moore, led his plane in an attack on two U-boats within twenty minutes of each other. Both were sunk. Moore was awarded an immediate Distinguished Service Order. His radio operator and navigator both received the Distinguished Flying Cross. One German submarine was sunk by a British warship, the destroyer escort *Affleck,* commanded by Captain Robert Lloyd. Four years earlier, at Dunkirk, when a sub-lieutenant, Lloyd had made three rescue journeys to and from the beach in a fishing boat. For his success on D-Day he was awarded a bar to his Distinguished Service Cross.

At 5.30 A.M. the warships of the Western (American) and Eastern (British) naval task forces, having navigated the ten lanes that had been cleared through the German minefields, began a sustained bombardment of the German coastal batteries and beach defenses. The closest ship was only two and a half miles offshore; the farthest, thirteen miles. For two and a half hours they kept up a relentless barrage of fire. (See the maps on pages 196 and 197.)

As day dawned off Sword and Juno Beaches, the two British midget submarines that had been off the coast of Normandy for three nights, struggling with their slow diving speed against a strong cross-tidal stream, rose to the surface and flashed their lights to seaward. They were in the correct position to mark the extremities of the landing area and to guide the oncoming assault craft. Immediately after the midget submarines, the first craft came in on Gold, Juno, and Sword, bringing, at first light, three battalions of British sappers. Going ashore at low tide, they used their explosives to make safe the thousands of mine-laden obstacles strewn on the beaches. Three-quarters of these men were killed by German machine-gun fire as they worked. There was nowhere they could take shelter on the vast expanse of sand if they were to complete their task. On the American beaches, Utah and Omaha, this dangerous, often fatal work was done by members of the Naval Combat Demolition Units (the NCDUs). They were among the first troops to go ashore at Utah—and also at Omaha.

Each demolition unit consisted of six or seven combat engineers and the same number of navy demolition experts.

Each unit was given a fifty-yard sector of the beach, charged with clearing their section of all German beach obstacles that would impede, or damage, the subsequent landing craft when the tide came in and covered the obstacles. These men went ashore from landing ships just after six o'clock. "On our way in," recalled Eugene D. Shales, then a nineteen-year-old sergeant, "we passed some landing crafts that may have encountered mines or been hit by German artillery. Floating bodies of GIs suddenly gave me a firsthand glimpse of what war is like." As well as full combat gear, the men of the demolition units carried satchels with explosives, detonators, and fuses. The fuses were protected from the water by latex condoms taped at the open end.

The demolition units placed their explosive charges on the back side of the obstacles, so that the explosions "would hurl the fragments seaward," Sergeant Shales later wrote. "It all worked out fairly smoothly. The job was finished around midmorning, but there was pain associated with it, due to the loss of a member of my squad, Leo Indelicato, who was killed by artillery fire during that task."

Another member of the demolition units at Utah Beach, John E. Dunford, was forced by German artillery fire to drop his explosive charges before he could set them. Taking refuge in a shell crater, he was hit. Two of his colleagues also were wounded. They made their way up the beach to a German pillbox that had been overrun and turned it into a first-aid station. "The beach was getting crowded. The ships were piling up as the infantry were coming in. An Army Engineer blew a hole in the seawall just east of the pillbox where I was sitting." Then the Germans began shelling again, and the wounded had to find somewhere else to shelter.

Another demolition man, James H. Burke, remembered the ten dead and twenty wounded among the demolition units on Utah Beach. "So it was difficult for us to accept the landing being called 'a piece of cake,'" he wrote, and added, "I have been trying to make people aware of this fact for years."

Preceding the troops on the two British beaches were men of the Landing Craft Obstacle Clearance Unit (LCOCU), the equivalent of the American demolition units. Drawn from the Royal Navy, the Royal Marines, and the Royal Engineers, they went ashore in rubber dinghies, wearing frogmen's suits, to place explosive charges against the larger beach obstacles. The first men to land on the beaches, they were confronted by deliberate German shooting, and accidental shooting from those making for the shore (now known as "friendly fire"). One of them later recalled the effect of the German snipers: "They were nipping us off as I was working with two blokes on a tough bit of element, when I suddenly found myself working alone. My two pals just gurgled and disappeared under the water."

Many thousands of mined obstacles having been cleared, the main landing forces approached their respective beaches. Off all the landing beaches the sea was rough, with waves almost everywhere three to four feet high. Many of the men in their landing craft had been seasick during the all-night crossing. The wind generally was force 4—between thirteen and eighteen miles an hour. But when the leading landing craft—including those carrying the amphibious DD tanks—touched down, it was, in Admiral Ramsay's words, "at the right place and at approximately the right time throughout the length of the front." At six-thirty in the morning, more than six hours after the first parachute landings, American troops landed at Utah Beach with their amphibious tanks. They were followed almost immediately by their fellow Americans landing at Omaha Beach.

At 7:25 A.M. the first British soldiers were ashore at Gold and Sword Beaches, followed, at Juno Beach, by the Canadians, the first 2,400 of the 15,000 who were to land that morning, supported by seventy-six amphibious tanks. Unlike the other Allied forces, the Canadians were almost all civilian volunteers.

Seasickness on the crossing was widespread at all the landings. The wind had whipped up rough seas and made the crossing a torment for many. "It wasn't too bad for us sailors," commented a Royal Navy Commando, Ronald McKinlay, "but I think one of the main reasons why Normandy was a great success was that the soldiers would much rather have fought thousands of Germans than go back into those boats and be seasick again."

At Juno, as on all the beaches, the warships offshore were starting their final hour of bombardment of the German batteries, in anticipation of the troops reaching them and advancing beyond them. Above the beachhead the Allied air forces flew a total of 13,688 sorties on June 6. These included reconnaissance flights above and beyond the beachhead, cross-Channel shipping protection, smokescreen cover, convoy and beach cover, artillery spotting, anti-U-boat patrols, parachutist and glider tugs, defensive patrols and offensive sweeps.

The German lacked the ability in the air to respond to the landings. When darkness fell, Allied night fighters patrolled above the shipping lanes and beachhead. To assist them, five tank landing ships had been converted into Fighter

Direction Tenders (FDTs), with radar apparatus set up on the deck, and Royal Air Force as well as Royal Navy personnel. For a week, these vessels remained off each of the beaches, guiding the Allied fighter force.

The night air defenses on D-Day had been planned at Montgomery's headquarters by his Anti-Aircraft Adviser, Brigadier Basil Hughes, an expert on the uses of radar, who was said to be able to walk into any radar cabin and diagnose its sets' faults at once. In the run-up to D-Day, Hughes had both planned and established the system of coordination between British and American anti-aircraft units.

The German navy was unable to halt or even harass the cross-Channel invading forces. Navy Group West, based at Cherbourg, consisted of only sixty craft, which were under continual Allied air attack. The destroyer flotilla had been reduced to two operational vessels. The Allied naval operations during June 6 were of great complexity and daring, the culmination of more than a year of intense preparation, no less complex or difficult than the air and land operations. In all, seven thousand Allied ships took part on D-Day. The written orders for their maneuvering in the crowded offshore waters of the landing areas, bringing the men to the shore and bombarding the German shore defenses, filled a thousand pages.

The largest component of Neptune was more than four thousand landing craft. Half of these, including the main tank landing craft (the LSTs), could travel under their own power. The others were taken across the Channel by armed salvage tugs and protected by armed trawlers. Almost all the LSTs had been built in the United States. Each could carry eighteen tanks or thirty trucks, or 500 to 1,400 tons of supplies. This landing craft armada was preceded by 287 minesweepers clearing a path for it and by 138 warships bombarding the German coastal defenses.

Churchill had hoped to witness the landings on D-Day from a warship offshore, but both the king and Eisenhower had dissuaded him. General de Gaulle had also hoped to go ashore, as France's liberator, as soon as possible. Both men had to wait, Churchill until D+6 and de Gaulle until D+8. It was not the visitors, however exalted, but the fighting men who were the focus of attention and bore the burden of fighting from the first hours, in the air, at sea, and on land.

10

D-Day:
Fighting on Land

Utah, Omaha, Gold, Juno, and Sword

British naval officers guided the soldiers on all the beaches. Among those officers was Captain Colin Madden, who a year earlier had brought a large flotilla of American-built landing craft across the Atlantic, via Bermuda and Gibraltar. On D-Day, Madden, on board the American escort vessel *Lawford*, was responsible for the accurate arrival of the 3rd Canadian Brigade on Juno Beach.

Offshore, the tanks, men, and supplies of each LST were unloaded either directly onto the beach or onto a "Rhino" ferry, on which they would be motored to the beach—the Rhino ferries having been towed across the Channel by the LSTs. Sometimes mistakes occurred: when one Rhino pilot saw a soldier on the beach frantically waving a red light at him and shouting, he assumed that the soldier was indicating the spot where he had to land the craft. The soldier was, however, trying to warn the pilot of the presence of a mine at that spot on the shoreline. The landing craft hit the mine, and several vehicles were damaged and men injured.

As the soldiers reached the shore, they emerged from their landing craft and strode—or stumbled—forward through what they hoped would be cleared sections of the beach. This was often not so, and many became casualties at the moment of landing and in the first minutes afterward, amid continuous fire from the German batteries, German pillboxes, and German snipers. Still, within a few hours, the men almost everywhere overran the beaches and established themselves there as yet more men landed and pushed forward.

Each of the five landing beaches—Utah, Omaha, Juno, Gold, and Sword—had its own tales of struggle and endurance, or setbacks and successes. On Utah, as on Sword Beach, it was the parachutists who had begun the assault, while it was still dark. The task was entrusted to men of the 101st Airborne Division, the "Screaming Eagles," and the 82nd Airborne Division. Of the 6,600 men of the 101st who dropped that night, starting an hour and a half after midnight in thick cloud and bad weather, only 1,100 reached their reporting points at dawn. A further 1,400 had reached their dawn destinations by the end of the day. The rest had come down too far from their dropping zones to reach their battle stations. But a sufficient number were in place, or knew what to do although in the wrong place, to ensure that the exits leading from Utah Beach across flooded marshland were secured before the landings, ensuring that the troops could get ashore and move inland.

At the town of Sainte-Mère-Église, the objective of one of the 82nd Airborne Division dropping zones behind

Utah Beach, an Allied bombing raid shortly before midnight had set a large house on fire. As the mayor and villagers formed a long line to the village pump, and were passing buckets of water from hand to hand to throw on the flames, paratroopers began to fall "like human confetti" among them. German soldiers shot at the Americans as they fell. One parachutist, John Steele, caught by his parachute in the church steeple, feigned death to avoid being shot at. After two hours hanging there, he was cut down and taken prisoner.

Staff Sergeant Tom Rice of the 101st Airborne, who dropped in the most southerly zone, later recalled the final moments of the flight: "The sky was lit up bright as day—ack-ack bursts, streams of red, green, and white tracers converged on us and showery bursts of flares outlined us in the skies as we neared our drop zone." Rice was the first to drop from his plane. It was 1:31 A.M. "We were at about 350 feet then and going about 165 mph; couldn't slow down because we would be an easier target. Luckily I wasn't hit . . . I came in on a field that was spattered by canals. I didn't get wet even though my chute re-inflated and I was being pulled towards a canal. I cut the suspension line in time. I couldn't get out of my harness because I had so much equipment on, couldn't even get my weapon out. Finally had to cut my way out. We organized and raised hell behind enemy lines until the seaborne troops reached us."

Also dropping behind Utah Beach was Lieutenant Eugene D. Brierre. After landing, he was sent by General Maxwell Taylor on three patrols in the area of his drop. "We never did run into any live enemy," he recalled. "We did find many dead Germans. We cut off their insignia and brought these back to General Taylor." On his first patrol "I noticed a wedding band on a dead German. I never gave it another thought. On the second patrol I passed over the same location and saw that the finger had been cut off."

After the capture of Pouppeville, the nearest village to Lieutenant Brierre's drop and less than a mile from an imminent beach landing area, "I came into a house where a German was lying on the floor; his gun was near him. I almost shot him when I realized that he was seriously wounded. He signalled me to hand him something. I saw that he was pointing towards a rosary. I grabbed his gun and unloaded it and put it at the other side of the room. I then picked up the rosary and handed it to him. He had the look of deep appreciation in his eyes and began to pray, passing the beads through his fingers. I learned the following day that he died shortly after I discovered him."

Three hours after the first American parachutists had descended behind Utah Beach, men of the 3rd Battalion of the 505th Parachute Infantry Regiment—part of the 82nd Airborne and led by Lieutenant Colonel Edward C. Krause—entered Sainte-Mère-Église from their nearby dropping zones. The Germans withdrew. It was four-thirty in the morning. Krause hoisted the Stars and Stripes on the church steeple. The Americans had liberated a town in France for the first time since 1918.

There were setbacks at Utah, as on every beach. Of the 360 United States bombers sent just before the landings to bomb the German beach defenses at Utah, 67 did not release their bombs: visibility was too bad. When, at three-thirty in the morning, the men transferred while at sea from their transport ships to their landing craft, many, falling in the heavy swell from the rigging on which they were descending to the landing craft, broke their legs: their equipment weighed almost seventy pounds. Landing three hours later, they discovered that they were more than a mile south of where they should have been. It was the assistant divisional commander, Brigadier General Theodore Roosevelt Jr.—a son of President Theodore Roosevelt and cousin of Franklin Roosevelt—who, having landed with the first wave of the attacking forces, took charge. Rather than reembark and move to the correct landing area, he decided to move inland. Striding up and down the beach, cane in hand, he urged the men forward.

For his actions on Utah Beach, General Roosevelt was awarded the Medal of Honor, one of four awarded on D-Day. His citation notes that despite his high rank, "he personally led a number of groups of soldiers from the beach, over the seawall, and to positions inland where they could establish themselves. . . . Under his seasoned, precise, calm, and unfaltering leadership, assault troops reduced beach strong points and rapidly moved inland with minimum casualties. He thus contributed substantially to the successful establishment of the beachhead in France." It was General Roosevelt who led the attack on Blockhouse W5, which Rommel had inspected a month earlier. By chance, the men came ashore in an area less heavily defended than the one where they were intended to land.*

General Roosevelt died of a heart attack shortly after the Utah landings. His brother, an aviator, had been killed in action in the First World War. When the Second World War American National Cemetery was created on the bluff

---

*The reverse had happened during the Gallipoli landings in 1915, when the current had taken the main Australian and New Zealand (Anzac) troops too far north, from the intended, and gently sloping, landing beach to a steep incline at the base of steep cliffs (Anzac Cove).

above Omaha beach, his brother's body was brought from elsewhere in France and reburied next to him. Thirty other pairs of brothers lie side by side in that cemetery. Another eight pairs of brothers are also buried there but in different rows. A father and son also lie side by side, Colonel Ollie Reed and his son Ollie Reed Jr., both killed in Normandy.

One of the main German defenses at Utah Beach was the St-Marcouf Battery at Crisbecq. In the early morning hours of June 6 some six hundred bombs were dropped on it without destroying it, so strong were the concrete casemates, two of them only completed within a week of D-Day.

A force of three hundred German soldiers defended the battery. Early that morning, while it was still dark, twenty American parachutists who landed nearby—many miles from their dropping zone—were taken prisoner. When daylight came the battery opened fire on the invasion fleet. A destroyer was sunk and a cruiser damaged. The naval forces returned fire, their heavy naval guns destroying the main guns in the battery, although the concrete structures remained intact, and the soldiers inside them, protected by minefields, barbed wire, and seventeen machine guns, held out against the Americans for six days—long after the battle had moved several miles southward.

Among the men who participated in the action off Utah were eight hundred Danes, mostly sailors serving on board ship. Denmark had been under German occupation since April 1940. Many of the Danes who escaped joined the British forces. One, a member of the Special Boat Service, Captain Anders Lassen, was to win a posthumous Victoria Cross a month before the end of the war.

On Utah Beach, the wounded John Dunford had watched on the shore as German prisoners were rounded up "and put into a barbed-wire area." It was five or six in the afternoon. "I got myself down to the shore to the ships that would carry the wounded and prisoners of war back to England." As he went in and out of consciousness, the ship "headed back across the Channel."

Between Omaha and Utah Beaches was a cliff promontory, Pointe du Hoc, four miles beyond the most westerly landing area of Omaha. The six heavy guns of its fortified battery, each of which was believed by the Allies to have a range of 25,000 yards, were a threat to both Utah and Omaha Beaches. The battery had been attacked throughout May by daylight bombing and then by both day and night bombing on June 2, 3, and 4. Aerial reconnaissance showed that enormous damage had been done. But to be certain, a further bombing raid was carried out on the night of June 5–6, followed by a commando raid by men of the 2nd Ranger Battalion. They began the attack at dawn, determined to scale the hundred-foot cliff. Just before they attempted the climb, a raid by eighteen American bombers forced the defenders underground. Then, as the rangers began to climb the cliff, using ladders, they were given powerful and effective cover by two Allied warships, the American destroyer *Satterlee* and the British destroyer *Talybont*.

When the naval gunfire ceased, a few of the German defenders emerged from the bunkers, but were quickly killed or captured as the rangers reached the clifftop. There, they found that all but one of the much-feared heavy guns were not there. The one that remained had been damaged in an earlier air attack. The remaining five had been taken from their emplacements and hidden, unguarded, in a nearby orchard. The rangers destroyed them with grenades.

It was on Omaha Beach that the worst setbacks on D-Day took place. Problems began long before the troops landed. While still eleven miles offshore, the men going ashore were transferred from ships to their assault landing craft. This was twice the distance the British would use an hour later on their beaches, and it was against the advice of the British planners. Eleven miles involved a three- to four-hour journey to the beach. It was therefore still dark when the troops had to transfer to their landing craft in order to reach the shore at the correct time. Because of the dark, many landing craft, including those containing the engineers who would have to clear the beach obstacles, lost their correct positions in the armada.

The journey was not only longer than at any other beach but also fraught with the problems of a rough sea. "I never saw water that bad," recalled Sergeant Roy Stevens, "the seas were just rolling and rolling, and there were whitecaps way out where we were, twelve miles from the coast."

While the landing craft were still 6,000 yards offshore, twenty-nine floating tanks were launched, but many sank like stones, with their crews inside them. Only two reached the beach. The artillery needed on the beach had been loaded onto amphibious DUKWs. This made them topheavy, and they capsized. More than twenty artillery pieces went to the bottom of the sea.

Ten landing craft bringing in the infantry were swamped by the heavy seas and sank. The men, each carrying almost seventy pounds of equipment, had little chance of survival. Many of the landing craft that did reach the shore were off course and, because of the long journey, almost all of the men were cold, cramped, and seasick. Before they reached the shore, the Germans opened fire on them. Many were killed in the boats. Others drowned under the weight of their equipment as they struggled in deep water. Yet others were shot dead as they waded forward toward the beach.

An official American account records one episode, the story of Able Company's landing: "At exactly 6.36 A.M., ramps are dropped along the boat line and the men jump off in water anywhere from waist deep to higher than a man's head. This is the signal awaited by the Germans atop the bluff. Already pounded by mortars, the floundering line is instantly swept by crossing machine gun fires from both ends of the beach." That particular company "has planned to wade ashore in three files from each boat, centre file going first, then flank files peeling off to right and left. The first men out try to do this but are ripped apart before they can make five yards. Even the lightly wounded die by drowning, doomed by the waterlogging of their overloaded packs."

The official account continues: "Already the sea runs red. Even among some of the lightly wounded who jump into shallow water, the hits prove fatal. Knocked down by a bullet in the arm or weakened by fear and shock, they are unable to rise again and are drowned by the onrushing tide. Other wounded men drag themselves ashore and, on finding the sands, lie quiet from total exhaustion, only to be overtaken and killed by the water. A few move safely through the bullet swarm to the beach, then find that they cannot hold there. They return to the water to use it for body cover. Faces turned upward, so that their nostrils are out of the water, they creep toward the land at the same rate as the tide. That is how most of the survivors make it. The less rugged or less clever seek the cover of enemy obstacles moored along the upper half of the beach and are knocked off by machine gun fire. Within seven minutes after the ramps drop, Able Company is inert and leaderless."

A member of one of the demolition units on Omaha Beach, Michael A. Accordino, had watched as the ramp of an infantry landing craft received a direct hit, "killing a few of the men, and the rest of the men rushed off, leaving those killed draped over the rail. It was a sad sight to see that happen," and he added, "I lost nine of my friends that day."

In midmorning, two Allied destroyers, coming to within a thousand yards of Omaha Beach, shelled the German positions that were still firing onto the beach. During the day, the 3rd Platoon of the 607th Graves Registration Company went ashore, to set up a body collection point on the beach. Under cover of the destroyers' fire, two Engineer Combat Battalions bulldozed two gaps in the dunes, filled in the antitank ditch, and cleared the minefields. Thirty-five of them were killed; among them were two brothers, Jay B. Moreland and William W. Moreland, whose bodies were never found.

For making it possible for the troops to move off the beach, the men of the Engineer Combat Battalions were collectively awarded the Croix de Guerre. As French troops were not to land in Normandy for several more days, these Americans were the first combat troops to receive this high French decoration on French soil since 1940.

Among those killed on Omaha Beach were nineteen of the thirty-four soldiers from a single town, Bedford, Virginia. No other community in the United States—or in Britain—lost such a high proportion of soldiers on D-Day. Reflecting on losses at Omaha, where an estimated 2,000 American soldiers were killed—most of them while they were trying to land—Eisenhower later revealed that the German resistance there "was at about the level we had feared all along the line." Yet only at Omaha had the German defenders been able to pin down the American assaulting force, of nearly 35,000 men, to a perimeter no more than a mile deep.

The landing on Juno Beach was carried out by Canadian troops, 15,000 in all, three times the number who landed at Dieppe in 1942. Among the five cruisers bombarding the German positions during the Juno landing was the Polish cruiser *Dragon*. Among the thirteen destroyers were two Canadian destroyers, *Algonquin* and *Sioux*. A French destroyer, *la Combattante*, also was in action that day off Juno Beach. Eight months later she sank in the North Sea, with the loss of sixty-five French and two British sailors.

At five-thirty in the morning, two hours before the landings were to begin at Juno, four German torpedo boats appeared out of the smoke screen laid by Allied aircraft between the German batteries at Le Havre and the bombarding battleships. The boats fired their torpedoes and sped back to their base at Le Havre. Only one torpedo found its mark, sinking the Royal Norwegian Navy's destroyer *Svenner*. The Norwegian crew saved themselves by jumping into the sea.

As at Utah and Omaha, so at Juno, the sea had been rough, and many of the men were seasick long before they reached the shore. Once there, the noise of the air and sea bombardments was almost overwhelming. But there were moments of relief. Gordon Hendery, who commanded three of the landing craft at Juno Beach, on which soldiers of the Canadian Scottish and Nova Scotia regiments were sailing, later recalled, "A wonderful thing happened. All of a sudden one of the lads, a sergeant, got up and started singing 'Roll out the Barrel.' Just for a moment, the fear from their faces left, and we all sang together."

The German defensive positions at Juno Beach had not been as badly damaged by the air and sea bombardments as the invaders had intended. Ingenuity often prevailed where preparation could not: in one instance on the beach, the driver of a bulldozer silenced a German pillbox by lumbering up behind it and filling it with sand.

The Canadian troops persevered, and by ten-thirty that morning a group of journalists was able to set up its headquarters in a hotel at Bernières. A plaque on the building records: "The first HQ for journalists, photographers and moviemakers, British and Canadian, from which the first reports destined for the Press of the free world were despatched." An hour later the commander of the Canadian troops, Major General R. F. L. Keller, left his headquarters ship and went ashore. That afternoon he held his first conference on French soil.

By the end of the day the Canadians on Juno had penetrated seven miles inland, farther than any other invading force. Ironically, they might have reached their objective, the airport at Carpiquet, on the outskirts of Caen, had not their successful advance created a massive traffic jam of men and equipment trying to move inland from the beach. Among the Canadian dead in action that day were twenty-one men from a single small town, London, Ontario, all serving in the First Hussars. Five days later the First Hussars were to lose sixty-one men in action farther inland.

.   .   .

Six thousand British troops landed on Gold Beach on the morning of D-Day. The main objective of the landing was to capture the town of Bayeux and the high ground east and west of it. At first there were setbacks. In the central sector the wind was so fierce—at force 5, the strongest in any sector of the D-Day landings—with waves more than four feet high, and the tide flowing so strongly that much of the supporting armor failed to come ashore as planned. Several amphibious tanks were lost before reaching the shore. On one sector, three of the landing craft of the Royal Marine Commandos were sunk when their landing craft hit three German obstacles. Forty-three marines died.

Among those crossing the beach to the seawall under heavy mortar and machine gun fire were Captain F. H. Honeyman, Lance Sergeant H. Prenty, and Lance Corporal A. Joyce. For their courage on the beach assault, Honeyman was awarded the Military Cross and Prenty and Joyce the Military Medal. All had to be awarded posthumously: the three men were killed in action five days later.

During the assault on the Gold Beach defenses at Mont Fleury, Company Sergeant Major Stanley Hollis was awarded the Victoria Cross—the only VC awarded on D-Day—for rushing at a German pillbox whose occupants were able to shoot in the rear of the advancing British troops. Hollis fired his Sten gun into it, jumped on top of it, recharged his Sten gun, threw a grenade through the door, killed two Germans, and took the remaining twenty-six Germans prisoner. Later that day, in the village of Crépon, two miles farther inland, Hollis rescued two of his men who were trapped in a house by creating a distraction, whereby he went forward firing a Bren gun in full view of the Germans who were firing at him and thus distracted did not see the two men as they made their way back to the British lines.

Once the troops were ashore at Gold, the radios in the headquarters of a leading battalion were destroyed by German artillery fire, making it impossible for the battalion to call for supporting fire from ships or aircraft. But the setbacks on the beachhead were overcome by continuing fierce assault by the troops ashore. German strong points were captured, and a German tank attack was beaten off. Reaching Arromanches from the land side, British troops had the small port under their control by late afternoon, making it secure for the arrival of the Mulberry harbor.

That afternoon, fearing a German counterattack, the British commanders on Gold did not push their men forward to their objective, Bayeux, which remained in German hands. But the beachhead was secured. That evening the first Mulberry harbor set sail from Britain en route for its place off Arromanches. Its structures were towed across the Channel by 150 tugs—British, American, and Dutch—their funnels marked "M" for Mulberry.

At Sword Beach, where the city of Caen was the day's objective, it was sixteen minutes past midnight when the first British gliders—having been towed over the Channel by Halifax bombers and released at 8,000 feet over the Normandy coast—began to land on target near the River Orne and Orne Canal bridges.

The first man to reach the ground was Major John Howard, of the Ox and Bucks Light Infantry. Four minutes later, pathfinder parachutists landed in the area to mark the dropping zones for other glider landings. The first of these parachutists to land was Lieutenant Robert de Latour. He was killed two weeks later.

At the Orne Canal, the attack on the bridge was led by Lieutenant Dan Brotheridge, who had landed with his thirty men in No. 1 glider. The bridge was captured, but Brotheridge was killed, his tombstone in the nearby cemetery at Ranville describing him as the first English soldier to fall in action. He was twenty-nine years old. On his gravestone are the words "Out of the bitterness of war, He found perfect peace." Next to him in the cemetery is the grave of an unknown German soldier. The capture of the Orne Canal bridge forced the local German company commander at Bréville, on his journey to warn his company headquarters a mere ten minutes away across the bridge, to make a six-hour detour through Caen.

On the eastern flank of Sword, Canadian troops in the 3rd Parachute Brigade—members of the 1st Canadian Parachute Battalion—were on a bridge-destroying mission, landing near Varaville and Robehomme at two-thirty in the morning. Although, like so many parachutists that day, they dropped over a much wider area than planned, they were able to regroup and carry out their assignment, blowing up the bridges over the River Dives. In the small village churchyard of Toufreville is the grave of Corporal E. O'Sullivan, killed that day. He was twenty years old. The village has named the church square after him. Another of the Canadian parachutists, Dennis Flynn, was wounded during the attack. After a period in the hospital he rejoined the paratroopers and jumped again in March 1945, during Operation Varsity, the crossing of the Rhine. On that occasion his leg was shattered by German machine-gun fire as he was escorting two German prisoners back across the river. He later used to say that he had only made three parachute jumps in his life: one for practice, one on D-Day, and one across the Rhine.

During the Canadian parachute landings near Varaville, two parachute transport aircraft were shot down near the village of Grangues. All six aircrew and nineteen parachutists were killed. A second aircraft crash-landed less than a hundred yards from the first. Four aircrew and four parachutists were killed, and the others were badly injured. The château near to which the planes had crashed was occupied by the Germans, who took the wounded survivors of the second plane to a stable block. They were joined in captivity by the survivors of a glider that crashed nearby. In all, forty-four soldiers, sailors, and airmen had been killed. Later that day, eight of the prisoners of war were shot. The Germans told the villagers that there had been an attempted breakout. The eight were buried in a trench—and in 1945 were identified by a British medical team.

The British glider-borne troops who had seized the Orne bridges shortly after midnight were reinforced within an hour by parachutists. Strong winds blew many off course, but their commanding officer, the unfortunately named Lieutenant Colonel Geoffrey Pine-Coffin, instructed his bugler to rally as many men as possible; some two hundred answered the call. By three in the morning they had established a perimeter around the two crossings.

German soldiers fought tenaciously from the first moments of the glider and parachute landings. But they were unable to prevent British glider and parachute troops breaking into the battery at Merville, a mile inland and with a field of fire over the beach. The men of the 9th Parachute

Battalion had dropped twenty minutes past midnight, many falling far from their dropping zone. By 2:20 in the morning, only a quarter of the six hundred who had dropped two hours earlier had reached the area where they were meant to be prior to the assault. Their commander, Lieutenant Colonel Terence Otway, who had landed in the correct area, was determined to reach the objective. Setting off with all the men he could muster, he reached the battery at Merville at 4:20 A.M. A fierce fight ensued and the battery was overrun. Forty minutes later Otway signaled his success to Major General Richard ("Windy") Gale, his divisional commander, by smoke flares and carrier pigeon. When the battery was examined, it emerged that the heavy guns believed to be there—with their power to bombard the beachhead— had never been installed.

With the battery at Merville overrun, the Germans concentrated on holding the village of Ranville, five miles inland. Within hours, however, they were driven out. Today, a plaque by the village church records that Ranville was the first French village to be liberated. Four years of Nazi rule were over, and General Gale took up his headquarters in a nearby château.

The Germans were determined not to give up. Later in the day they regained the battery at Merville, holding it until the following day, when it was taken by troops of No. 3 Commando. When men of the 21st Panzer Division attacked the Orne Canal bridge during the afternoon of D-Day, they were driven off by Major John Howard's glider troops and by parachutists, who had landed later in the morning. The paratroopers on the eastern flank of Sword Beach fought without respite for twenty-one hours against determined German opponents before securing the areas around their landing and dropping zones. General Gale later reflected: "The men were tired but well satisfied and proud of their achievements."

For the airborne commandos having secured the two Orne bridges and the battery at Merville, and having destroyed the bridges over the River Dives, the moment had come for the landings themselves. Among the troops who had crossed the Channel through the night and who fought their way ashore were the five hundred men of No. 4 Commando, who landed at 8:20 A.M. They were the first men to come ashore on Sword Beach. Many had suffered severe seasickness on the voyage over, first in two steamers and then in their landing craft. One of their officers, Major Patrick ("Pat") Porteous, had won a Victoria Cross at Dieppe. The boat he was in had been taking in water with every wave. "Approaching the beach all hell going on," he later wrote, "but anything preferable to this horrible boat. As the front ramps went down, she finally sank in three feet of water."

At 8:40 A.M., twenty minutes after the men of No. 4 Commando had come ashore, they were followed by Brigadier the Lord Lovat and No. 6 Commando. Lovat was the first to reach the shore, followed by Piper Bill Millin, who later described their arrival. "Lovat got into the water first . . ." Millin recalled. "I followed closely behind him . . . he's a man about six feet tall and, of course, the water came up to his knees. . . . I thought it would be all right for me so I jumped into the water and it came up to my waist . . . anyway I managed to struggle forward and then I started to play the bagpipes. I played 'Highland Laddie' towards the beach, which was very much under fire. At that time there were several . . . three . . . burning tanks, there were bodies, lying at the water's edge, face down floating back and forward. Some were frantically digging in . . . others crouched behind a low sea wall. No one could get off the beach. The road and the exits were under heavy fire."

Millin then made for cover at one of the exits from the beach, "a narrow road," as he recalled, "and I just got there behind a group of soldiers and they were all cut down . . . about nine or twelve of them . . . they were shouting and seeing me with the kilt and the bagpipes they shouted, 'Jock! Get the medics.' Then I looked around and to my horror I saw this tank coming off a landing craft with the flails going and making straight for the road. I tried to catch the commander's attention . . . his head was sticking out of the turret . . . but he paid no attention and went straight in and churned all the bodies up."

While the commandos were still at the water's edge, lying down, Lovat asked Millin to play. "That sounded rather ridiculous to me," Millin recalled, "to play the bagpipes and entertain people just like on Brighton sands in peacetime. Anyway . . . I started the pipes up and marched up and down. The Sergeant came running over, 'Get down, you mad bastard. You're attracting attention on us.' Anyway I continued marching up and down until we moved off the beach."

Soon after landing, No. 4 Commando overcame the German defenders, regrouped, and moved into the town of Ouistreham. There the German strong point—centered on the casino—was captured by Free French troops of No. 10 Inter-Allied Commando, thus enabling the troops in Ouistreham to advance inland. The Commando's own account recorded how heavy casualties were inflicted on the Germans, "who put up stiff resistance from strong fortifications and cunningly camouflaged blockhouses." The German concrete gun emplacements "had withstood the terrific air and naval bombardment extremely well and severe fighting took place," before their positions became untenable "and several surrendered"—the first German prisoners of war in Overlord.

Landing with No. 4 Commando was a Reuters war correspondent, Doon Campbell. Because he had been born with the lower part of his left arm missing, he was ineligible for military service. Crouching in a ditch for three hours, he typed out his dispatches from Normandy with his right hand. He was to stay with the front-line troops through France, Belgium, and Germany, sending his paper an eyewitness account of the liberation of Belsen concentration camp in April 1945.

Men and machines came ashore at Sword Beach throughout the day. Alf Freeman, a gunner on a motorized antitank gun, recalls how he and the other crewmen of their 17-pounder gun "were told that we might be landing in six feet or more of water, so we had to what they called 'jelly up' the engine, and we had to cover all the electrical parts, the plugs, the distributor, the leads, and the carburetor. It so happens we were very lucky, because when we drove down the ramp of the Tank Landing Boat into the water it was only two or three feet deep, and as the motor was very high with high wheels with thick treads the water hardly touched the engine. We drove up the beach between two white tapes onto the Normandy land."

Offshore, a French cruiser, *Courbet,* was one of the ships that had been towed across the Channel, without engine or guns, but filled with concrete, to make up the Gooseberry breakwater needed to provide protection for the landing craft. She was one of the warships that had taken part in the Anglo-French naval attack on the Dardanelles in 1915. In June 1940 she had helped the British evacuation from Cherbourg by providing cover with her guns. Off Sword Beach, immobile, she flew the French Tricolor and the Free French Cross of Lorraine. The Germans, believing that she was able to fight, shelled her continually, and even attacked her with human torpedoes. They were sustained in their belief that she was still a fighting ship by ships of the Allied naval force, which fired from behind her onto the German shore batteries.

At Lion-sur-Mer, between the British and Canadian beachheads, the German defenders had held up an advance by No. 41 Royal Marine Commando, which had the task of linking the two beachheads. Naval gunfire was unable to dislodge the Germans, who were still holding their position at the end of the day.

A German strong point two and a half miles inland from Sword Beach, a concrete bunker known to the attackers as "Hillman," was holding up the advance. It took six hours for the British to overcome the defenders. Twenty of the attackers—men of the Suffolk Regiment—were killed in the assault. The extra forces sent to capture Hillman diverted armor from the push toward Caen. As part of that push, at one in the afternoon a ten-minute British incendiary bomb raid on Caen led to many civilian deaths. At 4:25 P.M. the British launched another incendiary raid. Yet more citizens were killed, and the funeral parlor at which the municipality had stored five hundred coffins for "serious emergencies" was reduced to ashes. The deputy mayor noted in his diary, "We won't have a single coffin to bury the dead."

The Germans did not abandon Caen, despite the bombardment. To prevent a French uprising, they executed more than eighty members of the French Resistance who were being held as hostages in the Caen prison.

Caen was not to fall to the Allied forces that day—indeed, it was to remain in German hands for more than a month. By dusk on D-Day the nearest British troops were still four miles short of their objective. Then, at seven in the evening the Germans counterattacked, Panzer troops advancing toward the beaches and reaching the Channel coast at a point between the British and Canadian beaches. Had Rommel been at his headquarters that day, perhaps this crack unit would have been sent forward sooner. But news of the Allied landings had not reached him until ten-fifteen in the morning—more than three hours after the Americans had begun to fight their way ashore. He immediately flew back to France, having been instructed by Hitler to drive the invaders "back into the sea" by midnight. By midnight, however, 155,000 Allied troops were ashore.

Six German tanks reached the Channel coast that evening, at a point still patrolled by German units and defended by German coastal guns. But as more tanks hurried forward to join them, they were the victims of a freak mistake. Across their path, flying from west to east, came the massed ranks of the Allied planes and gliders of the 6th Airlanding Brigade, part of the 6th Airborne Division. These troops were flying to a landing point five miles farther east. But the Panzer commander convinced himself that this mass of men were aimed at him, and that this was a deliberate "overhead counterstroke." He therefore withdrew, leaving the six tanks that were already at the coast exposed and stranded.

The coast would have been impossible for the Germans to hold for long. The firepower of the British naval guns was massive. One 15-inch naval gun that brought death and destruction to the defenders on and behind Sword Beach had last been fired in anger at the Battle of Jutland in 1916. Hundreds of German soldiers were killed by these distant shells, against which they had no defense.

The German Air Force was unable to help the Panzers. Whereas the Allies flew 10,000 air sorties on D-Day, the German Air Force, which had once seen itself as the spearhead of the invasion of Britain, flew only 319 sorties, shooting down only one Allied plane. But the Panzers did not give up. Two miles inland, near Douvres-la-Délivrande, was a strongly fortified German radar station. Here the Panzers gathered, and here they fought with no intention of pulling back. They were not to be driven out of this strong point for another eleven days, becoming a thorn in the side of the advancing troops. But eventually they were overwhelmed.

In the nearby military cemetery are row upon row of German graves. Also in this cemetery lies a soldier from Lancashire, Gunner Clayton. Fifty years later Gunner Connell, who had been at his side when Clayton was killed, made his first ever pilgrimage back to Normandy. At the graveside he spoke two words, "My pal," and stood in silent remembrance.

On the night of June 6 the London *Evening News* told its readers in a confident headline: MONTY LEADS INVASION. TANKS PUSH ON PAST CAEN. This was not so. The Germans still held Caen and were determined not to give it up. At nine-thirty that evening Montgomery, Commander-in-Chief of the forces already ashore and those preparing to land in the days ahead, crossed the Channel on a British destroyer. He did not land but went to see his two commanders, General Bradley and General Dempsey, who were on board ship, offshore. Then Montgomery slept on a Royal Navy destroyer.

Despite the hard fighting on the beaches, the Allied casualties on D-Day were relatively low. Of the 150,000 men who parachuted, glided, or came in by sea, an estimated 4,572 were killed.* Churchill confided to Stalin: "We had expected to lose 10,000 men." In the First World War, on the first day of the Battle of the Somme, 20,000 men had been killed. Among the dead on D-Day were 359 Canadians; in 1942 more than 900 Canadians had been killed at Dieppe.

The first news of the Normandy landings reached German Supreme Headquarters in Berchtesgaden at about three o'clock on the morning of June 6. Hitler was not woken up. Three hours later, as more and more information was telephoned through, General Gunther Blumentritt, the Chief of Staff to the Commander-in-Chief West (von Rundstedt), informed General Warlimont that "in all probability this was the invasion and that Normandy was apparently the area."

Recognizing the seriousness of the landings, General Blumentritt urged, on behalf of von Rundstedt, that the reserves being held by the Armed Forces High Command (OKW), consisting of four motorized or armored divisions, should be released from their assembly areas and ordered to

---

*Estimates vary. Professor George J. Winter, after considerable research into the figures, gives them as: 2,500 Americans, 1,641 Britons, 359 Canadians, 37 Norwegians, 19 Free French, 13 Australians, 2 New Zealanders, and 1 Belgian.

positions closer to the beaches. General Warlimont immediately telephoned General Jodl, head of the Operations
Branch of the German Armed Forces High Command. "It
was soon clear," Warlimont wrote, "that Jodl was fully up to
date with all the information, but in the light of the latest
reports was not yet fully convinced that here and now the
real invasion had begun. He did not therefore consider that
the moment had arrived to let go our last reserves," and felt
that von Rundstedt must "first try to clear up the situation"
with Rommel's forces. This would give time, Jodl considered, "to get a clearer picture whether the operation in
Normandy was not a diversionary attack prior to the main
operation across the Straits of Dover."

Warlimont added that Jodl made this decision "on his
own responsibility, in other words without asking Hitler;
forever after it was the cause of the most bitter accusations
against OKW. The German defeat in Normandy with all its
fatal consequences was, people said, primarily due to this
failure to release the OKW reserves."

It was not until 10.30 A.M. that Rommel's headquarters
staff at la Roche-Guyon considered the situation suffi-
ciently definite to inform Rommel, who was still in
Germany. Three other senior officers were also far from
their posts: General Schlieben, commander of the fortress of
Cherbourg, was at a training course in Rennes; General
Feuchtinger, commander of the 21st Panzer Division—the
best troops in Normandy—was on vacation in Paris,
together with his Chief of Operations.

Throughout the morning of June 6 the various portions
of German Supreme Headquarters at Berchtesgaden
remained in touch with each other by telephone only.
General Jodl with his aides was in the small Reich

Chancellery there. Jodl's staff was in another building. Hitler was at the Berghof. It was not until midday that the senior officers at Berchtesgaden gathered for Hitler's daily briefing conference. But on that particular day the conference was not to take place at Berchtesgaden, where all the relevant military personnel were readily available, but an hour away by road, at Klessheim Castle, north of Salzburg.

The reason for this change of venue was that Hitler was awaiting a Hungarian State Visit. The Hungarian Prime Minister, General Döme Sztójay—a former Hungarian Military Attaché in Berlin—was to be received in style. Because of the news coming from Normandy, the briefing—which when official visitors were present was never more than a formal "showpiece"—was preceded by a preliminary conference in a room next to the entrance hall of the castle. The need for a guiding hand was urgent.

"I and many of the others were keyed up as a result of the portentous events which were taking place," General Warlimont recalled, "and as we stood about in front of the maps and charts we awaited with some excitement Hitler's arrival and the decisions he would make. Any great expectations were destined to be bitterly disappointed. As often happened, Hitler decided to put on an act. As he came up to the maps he chuckled in a carefree manner and behaved as if this was the opportunity he had been waiting so long to settle accounts with his enemy. In unusually broad Austrian he merely said, "So, we're off." After short reports on the latest moves by ourselves and the enemy we went up to the next floor where the 'showpiece' was laid on for the Hungarians." Warlimont added that "the usual overestimates of German forces and confidence in 'ultimate victory' were more than normally repellent."

Hitler, convinced that the Normandy landing was not the "real" Second Front, hesitated to commit his full resources to the bridgehead. During June 6, top-secret orders were sent out to all German naval units, warning them to be prepared for surprise attacks elsewhere than in Normandy. This message was decrypted at Bletchley that evening, giving the Allied commanders some assurance that even on June 7, D-Day plus one, the full force of German military might would not be thrown against them.

D-Day saw the launching of Operation Houndsworth, when two members of the British Special Air Service (SAS), Johnny Cooper—it was his twenty-fourth birthday—and Reg Seekings, were dropped in the Morvan region of France as the advance party for "A" Squadron of the 1st Special Air Service Regiment. Their instructions were to set up a base between the Loire and Dijon, establish contact with the French Resistance, arm and train them, and help them disrupt German lines of supply and French railway lines, to slow down the move of reinforcements to the Normandy beachhead. They began their task within hours of landing.

Inside France, almost thirty thousand Resistance fighters were awaiting the call to arms, having been massively equipped by British air drops. Among their weapons were tens of thousands of Sten guns and a quarter of a million grenades. As news of the Allied landings reached them, on clandestine radios and by word of mouth, the Resistance fighters collected their arms from their hidden depositories and began their acts of sabotage against the rail network vital for the movement of German troops to the battlefield.

· · ·

For many, D-Day was not only a turning point but also a moment of supreme relief. In the words of a fifteen-year-old Canadian schoolboy, Morley Wolfe, who had already joined the Royal Canadian Air Cadet Squadron, "For me on 6 June 1944, my war was over. No need for preparation or concern as to military service, only follow events to final victory."

11

Establishing the Beachhead

"Yesterday the great and dreadful day, that we have anticipated so long, dawned. I was up early, and heard the first news of the start of the invasion . . ." Abe Kramer, then serving in the Royal Air Force in Britain, wrote in his diary on the morning of June 7. "We were all very excited and thrilled and at the same time had heavy hearts when we thought of all those boys known and unknown to us, who are facing great danger and death."

In Italy, where the Allied soldiers had been fighting for almost a year, a British soldier recalled how "we didn't really discuss that this was truly the beginning of the end. Perhaps because the Allies had already breached Fortress Europe in 1943 in Sicily and Italy and had never looked back. We did speak in awe of how the first infantrymen must have felt as they approached the beaches."

That morning, readers of the morning newspapers in Britain were told, in an official government communiqué issued at midnight, how Allied invasion troops, "surging forward in mighty nonstop waves, have fought their way into Caen, fourteen miles from the coast. Heavy street fighting is going on." Like the report in the previous evening's British evening paper, this was untrue. The Germans in Caen were preparing for a long defense. Rommel had returned from Germany and was back at the beachhead, stiffening the morale of his troops, as he had done in North Africa two years earlier.

Hitler and Rommel were both convinced that the Normandy landings represented a feint and a trick. The best German spy in Britain—as Hitler regarded him—Juan Pujol Garcia, Germany's trusted Arabel (Britain's double agent Garbo)—reported that the real cross-Channel invasion was still to come, possibly near Calais, or near Dieppe, or even farther northeast, against the Belgian and Dutch coasts. As a result of Garcia's information, Hitler and Rommel agreed to keep substantial military forces—nineteen divisions in all, more than half a million men—ready to await the "real" invasion, 150 miles or more to the northeast of Normandy. The German soldiers facing the Allies at Normandy were thus denied the help of other soldiers who were waiting, inactive, for landings that never came. On June 7 Hitler gave orders to all German naval units to be prepared for an attack elsewhere.

In the early hours of June 7, to meet the attack in Normandy, German aircraft were ordered to the beachheads. Because the orders were sent by the most secret radio signals, the decrypters at Bletchley were in possession that same day of the details of these German aircraft transfers. In many cases the precise routes and destinations also were given, allowing the Anglo-American air forces to intercept them and shoot them down before they could reach the battle zone. Within four days, further Ultra decrypts enabled the Allies to track almost 300 of the 400 to 450 aircraft that were ordered to Normandy.

The secret Intelligence brought to Churchill on June 7 made it clear that the Germans remained convinced that Normandy was a feint and that the real landings would come later, elsewhere. As the Allies consolidated their positions on the Normandy beachhead that day and sought to enlarge them, the German Air Force High Command was warning its units in Western Europe that further landings could be expected either for a thrust toward Belgium, or in Norway, or near the port of Lorient on the French Atlantic coast, or on the western coast of the Cotentin Peninsula.

News of the Normandy landings spread rapidly throughout German-occupied Europe. During the morning of June 7 an Italian Jew, Primo Levi, who was then a slave laborer at the Buna synthetic-oil factory at Monowitz, near Auschwitz (the camp was known as Auschwitz III), was among thousands of Jewish slave laborers whose crushed spirits suddenly rose. While he watched, as he did every morning, a group of British prisoners of war marching from the adjacent camp on their way to work in the Buna factory, he noticed that there was "something different about them: they marched well aligned, chests thrust forward, smiling, martial, with a step so eager that the German sentinel who escorted them, a territorial no longer young, had difficulty keeping up with them. They saluted us with the V-sign of victory. The next day we found out that from a clandestine radio of theirs they had learned about the Allied landings in Normandy, and that was a great day for us, too: freedom seemed within reach."

Yet even as the Allies were gaining ground on the Normandy beaches, the SS were continuing the deportation of Jews to Auschwitz from France, Poland, Italy, Hungary, and Greece. But in Eastern Galicia—more than a thousand miles from Normandy—fifteen Jews in hiding were saved from discovery and death when the German soldiers stationed next to their hiding place—the attic of a large farm the soldiers had occupied—were transferred to the newly opened Western Front. "We saw the gates open. The Nazis went off with all their equipment. We could finally breathe as free people. We were saved, indirectly, by the Allied invasion of Normandy."

At Lion-sur-Mer a second attempt was made on June 7 to link the British and Canadian beachheads. Shortly before the men of No. 41 Commando, joined with infantrymen, were going to renew the attack on the German positions, three German planes—Heinkels—attacked with antipersonnel bombs, killing the Forward Observation Officer and wounding the commanding officer and eleven members of the headquarters staff. But by evening the German position had been overrun.

Also on June 7 a detachment of 47 Royal Marine Commando secured the link between the British on Gold Beach and the Americans on Omaha Beach. Within a week, Port-en-Bessin was serving as an important unloading base for Allied supplies, handling a thousand tons a day, far more than its prewar peacetime capacity. During June 7, Churchill telegraphed to Stalin about the larger harbor project, Mulberry: "Most especially secret. We are planning to construct very quickly two large synthetic harbours on the beaches of this wide, sandy bay of the Seine estuary. Nothing like these has ever been seen before. Great ocean liners will be able to discharge and run by various piers supplies to the fighting troops. This must be quite unexpected by the enemy, and will enable the build-up to proceed with very great independence of weather conditions."

On June 8, British troops from Gold Beach reached the American troops on Omaha Beach at Colleville-sur-Mer. "Overlord is a source of joy to us all," Stalin replied to Churchill on June 8. Above the battlefield the Germans had fewer than a hundred operational aircraft that day. On the ground, crucial top-secret orders were being decrypted. One decrypt enabled the British to pinpoint the exact location of the new headquarters of Panzer Group West. Two days later the headquarters, at la Caine, was an Allied bombing target. Four hundred bombs were dropped, and the headquarters staff was all but wiped out, seventeen officers being killed, including the senior officer, a major general. Not only did a Panzer counterattack being planned for June 11 have to be postponed for twenty-four hours, but also it became impossible to carry out Rommel's plan for a Panzer drive to the sea to split the Allied forces in two.

The Allies had another precious advantage, knowledge of German strategic thinking. Ultra messages studied by General Walter Bedell Smith at Allied Supreme Headquarters made clear, he noted on June 8, "the enemy's continuing belief that the present landings are soon to be followed by others, possibly in Norway, the Pas-de-Calais, the Low Countries, and elsewhere in France."

Strategic deception kept the Germans on the lookout for other invasion regions. Tactical deception caused them to be distracted from the true thrust of the battlefield. Operating in Normandy from the earliest days was Force R, commanded by David Strangeways—who had last seen France during the evacuation from Dunkirk. Strangeways had been brought by Montgomery from Italy in January 1944 to plan and take charge of tactical deception. He used Force R—a squadron of armored cars, several squadrons of field engineers, and an 880-strong special radio unit—to create the impression of a large military force against which considerable German diversions had to be made, to their serious disadvantage.

Aid to the French Resistance also continued. From the first days of Overlord, three-man inter-Allied Jedburgh teams—with British, American, and French officers working in tandem—were dropped throughout central France "to stimulate guerrilla action along the lines of communication." In all, ninety-three "Jeds," as they were known, were to be parachuted into France in the next few months.

Hitler and his senior Intelligence advisers remained convinced that Normandy was a diversion and that a further Western assault was imminent. On June 9, German Intelligence chiefs received, and at once passed on to Hitler, a message from Juan Pujol Garcia in Britain that after "consultation on 8th June in London with my agents Donny, Dick, and Dorick," he was of the opinion that the Normandy landings were "a diversionary manoeuvre designed to draw off enemy reserves in order to make a decisive attack in another place." These agents were figments of the imagination—and skillful creations—of the British Secret Service.

Arabel's report, Hitler was told by German Intelligence, "confirms the view already held by us that a further attack is to be expected in another place." That other place, German Intelligence felt, was possibly Belgium. Arabel's message, noted the head of the Intelligence Division of the German Armed Forces High Command on the bottom of it, "confirms the view already held by us that a further attack is to be expected in another place" and he added in brackets, "Belgium?"

Britain's double agent Garbo/Arabel had successfully maintained the Fortitude South deception three full days beyond the Normandy landings. Just over three years had passed since he had set up his Arabel network, with at various times twenty-seven spurious agents working under him. The characters and story of the three agents mentioned by Garbo on June 9 each had a carefully built-up history created by his British Intelligence handlers. "Donny," allegedly recruited in December 1943, was an ex-seaman and leader of the World Aryan Order. "Dick," recruited in February 1944, was "an Indian fanatic." "Dorick," also recruited in February 1944, was a disgruntled civilian living at the North Sea port of Harwich.

The senior officer at German Army Headquarters in Zossen, near Berlin, likewise felt that Normandy was only a diversion. "The main thrust," the Chief of the Army General Staff's Intelligence Division informed General Jodl on June 9, "must be expected at any moment in the Pas-de-Calais." That day, the German admiral commanding in the Atlantic suggested to his superiors that the "hesitant and slow" progress of the Allied landings in Normandy might indicate "an intended second landing at another point." This message was decrypted at Bletchley on June 10. Not only was deception continuing to keep a protective shield over the Allied armies but also the fact that the deception was working was known to the Allied commanders.

On June 9 the first Phoenix, the main element of the Mulberry artificial harbor, reached the coast off Arromanches. Within nine days, 115 Phoenixes had been sunk in a five-mile arc around Arromanches, enclosing two square miles of sea, approximately the size of Dover Harbor. (See the top map on page 204.) Barrage balloons and anti-aircraft guns defended the harbor from German air attack while it was under construction, but the German Air Force had been gravely weakened, and no serious attack was carried out as the artificial harbor began to take shape.

Four days after D-Day, on the morning of June 10, the fifty-mile length of the landing beaches was under Allied control, with territory held to a depth inland of between two and twelve miles. That day, 30 Assault Unit (30 AU) landed at Utah Beach. It was not an assault unit in the accepted sense of the word, but a set of teams that was to operate in German-held territory ahead of the main army, obtaining crucial German Intelligence documents on new weaponry and installations before the Germans could destroy them. The teams reported to an Intelligence unit in London headed by Commander Ian Fleming—later the author of the James Bond novels.

The Allies consolidated their landings and continued to advance inland despite another of Hitler's secret weapons, an unscupperable mine known to the Allies as the Oyster, and showing a technology far more advanced than the Allied mines. These Oysters had been laid surreptitiously off the Normandy beaches after D-Day, causing grave inconvenience by forcing ships to limit their speed to virtually one mile an hour to avoid detonating them. The new weapon was unable to make any serious inroads into Allied naval strength off the beaches, as the massive numerical superiority of the Allied naval forces enabled the losses to be sustained. Nor could the intrepid German sailors lay enough mines to make them a major hazard.

Everywhere on the battlefield, Allied forces met strong opposition, but Rommel knew its limitations, writing on June 10, "During the day practically our entire traffic—on roads, tracks, and in open country—is pinned down by powerful fighter-bomber and bomber formations, with the result that the movement of our troops on the battlefield is almost completely paralyzed, while the enemy can maneuver freely. Every traffic defile in the rear areas is under continual attack and it is very difficult to get essential supplies of ammunition and petrol up to the troops."

Rommel sought to focus his attacking forces against the American bridgehead in the Carentan-Montebourg area, to prevent the German forces in the Cotentin Peninsula from being cut off. Hitler, however, vetoed this plan and ordered Rommel to attack instead from Caen against the British bridgehead. The British troops, however, were reinforced more quickly than Rommel's and were able to advance against him before he was ready to attack.

German reinforcements brought in through Caen were to tie down the Allies in bloody fighting in the region that they had expected to overrun on their first day, and they were to prevent the Allies from breaking out. But by the night of June 10, more than 325,000 Allied soldiers were ashore on the Normandy beaches. The struggle ahead of them was to be fierce and prolonged, but the beachhead was secure, and the advance inland inexorable.

Ten days after the Normandy landings, Ultra decrypts made it clear that Hitler and his senior commanders were still convinced that the landings were part of an Allied deception plan, and that the real landings would come later, against the Pas-de-Calais, Belgium, or Holland. The art of strategic deception had found its finest hour.

12

Beyond the Point
of No Return

O n June 18 the British and American Mulberry harbors were both in place, off Omaha and Gold Beaches, ready to begin unloading several thousand tons of supplies a day over four miles of piers and ten miles of floating roadways. But on the day after they began operating there was a fierce storm, which continued for three days, and the harbor at Omaha—which had been somewhat hastily assembled—was completely destroyed. The harbor at Arromanches, although battered, was still operational, but the landing of men and supplies was severely affected for some weeks.

The Allied setback at the two Mulberry harbors was more than compensated for by the continuing German conviction, thanks to Garbo and his bogus fellow German agents, that the First United States Army Group was still gathered in Kent and East Anglia and ready to go into action. A German High Command map on June 19 showed British, American, and Canadian troops all in readiness, and located,

including the "28th American Motorized Infantry Division," carrying out assault training at Harwich, on the
North Sea coast. No such division and no such training
existed. Nor did any other other sixteen military formations
identified by German Intelligence. (See the map on page
203).

By June 20 half a million Allied soldiers were ashore. The
Germans held Caen, but the sheer weight of Allied airpower, and the daily growing number of men ashore, was
beginning to tell against them. Yet still the deception plan
was holding. On June 26, twenty days after the Normandy
landings, von Rundstedt was still referring to the "First
United States Army Group" as a serious and imminent
threat. It was, he said, ready to embark, and was—he was
convinced—even larger than Montgomery's 21st Army
Group then fighting in Normandy.

With the capture of Cherbourg on June 27, the army that
had landed in Normandy acquired its first major port. Two
days later, Rommel flew to Berchtesgaden to tell Hitler that
all was lost. Hitler promised him a special German bombing
offensive over the Normandy beachhead, and German torpedo boat and submarine attacks on the cross-Channel supply lines. Realizing that these measures were beyond
Germany's means, Rommel told him, "The whole world
stands arrayed against Germany, and this disproportion of
strength—" Before Rommel could finish his sentence,
Hitler interrupted him with the words "I think, Field Marshal, you had better leave the room!"

Returning to Normandy, Rommel learned that more
than 40,000 German soldiers were now prisoners of war. A
million Allied soldiers were ashore, and more than 170,000

vehicles—a veritable armada of tanks, armored vehicles, jeeps, and trucks. In addition, ten British and seven American airstrips were in operation in the beachhead. Although Caen was still under German control, elsewhere on the battlefield the Allied forces were almost twenty miles inland, with the Cotentin Peninsula securely under American control.

Starting on June 13 the flying bomb (the V-1), the first of Hitler's secret weapons, had been launched against London; and in September the rocket bomb (the V-2) followed. The V-bombs eventually killed more than two thousand Londoners, but they could not halt or set back the Normandy landings. Eisenhower later commented that had the V-bombs been available against the Normandy beaches—especially the V-2, with its one-ton warhead—they would have constituted a "formidable obstacle" to the landings.

In northern Europe the German High Command still expected the "main thrust" of the Allies to come elsewhere, perhaps near the mouth of the Seine, perhaps in Brittany. On July 4 Hitler was still being told by his experts that the real Allied attack might come elsewhere. Churchill told Eisenhower: "The forces in Britain are a dominant preoccupation of the Huns." But even Hitler admitted that if the Allies broke out of Normandy, Germany did not possess "any comparable tactical mobility."

That day, British bombers dropped 2,500 tons of bombs on Caen, as the first step in the city's capture. As many as three thousand French civilians were killed. While Caen fell to the Western Allies, Soviet troops entered Minsk, the capital of Byelorussia, taking 150,000 German soldiers captive. "The enemy is burning and bleeding on every front at once," Churchill telegraphed to Stalin, "and I agree with you that this must go on to the end."

On July 9, at his headquarters in la Roche-Guyon, Rommel received a senior member of the German Military Command in Paris, who told him of the plot to assassinate Hitler planned for three days' time. In the event, the attempt, which had to be postponed for another nine days, failed. Rommel, implicated in it, was given the choice of a public trial and execution, ór suicide and a state funeral. He chose suicide.

Hitler remained the arbiter of German war policy. He also remained convinced that the British and Americans were preparing a landing elsewhere in northern Europe. On July 24 the British Joint Intelligence Committee reported that Ultra decrypts showed that the Germans were "still apprehensive" of a second major landing somewhere between the River Seine and the Franco-Belgian frontier. The committee noted that there had been "no considerable transfer" of German forces from the Pas-de-Calais, which remained "strongly garrisoned."

To maintain the deception, those First United States Army Group officers who visited Normandy did so in strictest secrecy. Patton was one such visitor in July, together with one of his most senior officers, General Lesley McNair. On July 25, McNair was sheltering in a slit trench watching the start of a major American offensive. During the initial air bombardment, in which 2,340 aircraft dropped 4,000 tons of bombs and napalm, some of those bombs fell short: they were known then as "shorts," today as "friendly fire."

In all, 111 American soldiers were killed. Among the dead was McNair, whose body was thrown sixty feet in the air and was unrecognizable except for the three general's stars on his collar. To maintain the essential secrecy of the continuing Pas-de-Calais deception, McNair's funeral was conducted in strictest secrecy. Patton was one of the pall-bearers, noting in his diary: "A sad ending and a useless sacrifice." McNair was replaced in fortitude by a distinguished older general, John L. DeWitt, and the deception was maintained.

In the first two weeks of August a massive Allied thrust on all the fronts broke out of Normandy. Starting on August 7, Canadian troops drove toward Falaise, supported by a Polish armored division. On their flank, the British also advanced. American troops, from the base of the Cotentin Peninsula, swept westward to St-Malo, south to the River Loire, and east to Le Mans. Off Normandy, the Mulberry harbor at Arromanches had begun to work at full capacity, enabling 7,000 tons of war material to be landed every twenty-four hours. In the ten months during which the harbor was operational, two and a half million men, half a million vehicles, and four million tons of supplies were to reach the battlefield through it. On August 12 PLUTO (Pipe Line Under the Ocean) was laid across the Channel from Britain to Cherbourg, a distance of just over eighty miles. Within three weeks fuel oil was flowing eastward behind the advancing Allied tank and vehicle depots. In all, 172 million gallons flowed through the pipeline.

On August 15 the Allies launched Operation Dragoon, an amphibious landing on the French Riviera—which Churchill witnessed from on board ship—and which rapidly pushed northward. In Normandy, as the Allies drove toward the Seine, the German soldiers in the Falaise pocket were trapped and defeated. Visiting the battlefield, Eisenhower was shocked; it was, he later wrote, "unquestionably one of the greatest 'killing grounds' of any of the war areas. Roads, highways, and fields were so choked with destroyed equipment and with dead men that passage through the area was extremely difficult. Forty-eight hours after the closing of the gap I was conducted through it on foot, to encounter scenes that could be described only by Dante. It was literally possible to walk for hundreds of yards, stepping on nothing but dead and decaying flesh."

On August 25 Paris was freed after four years of German occupation. The liberation of three more capital cities, Brussels, The Hague, and Luxembourg, lay ahead of the troops who had landed in Normandy, as did the crossing of the Rhine and the surrender of the German forces. Those in northern Germany surrendered to Montgomery on Luneberg Heath on 4 May 1945; the rest of the German forces surrendered three days later at Reims, where General Bedell Smith signed for the Allied Expeditionary Forces.

Fighting in Western Europe would continue for eight months after the Normandy landings. The triumphant turning point of 6 June 1944 was also a prelude to much suffering and destruction in towns and villages from Normandy to the Baltic, and heavy loss of life, both of soldiers and civilians.

D-Day was a turning point created by a combination of politicians and planners, by leaders at every level focused intently on the challenging task, and by many millions of others: Ultra decrypters at Bletchley, inventors, organizers of special units, creators of deception, engineers and technicians, shipyard and factory workers, doctors and nurses, members of the French Resistance, and, on the beachhead itself, the soldiers, sailors, and airmen of all the Allied forces. Many of those soldiers, sailors and airmen lie today in war cemeteries throughout Normandy, where the graves of the dead of many nationalities—among them Americans, Britons, Canadians, Poles, Frenchmen, Belgians, Czechoslovaks, and Dutch—are to be found. There are also six German war cemeteries, and German graves in many Allied cemeteries.

The Normandy campaign was a victory for the Allies over the Axis, but the dead know no nationality. Those who helped to secure victory in Normandy, and who survived, did not always sleep untroubled by their memories of the pain and suffering of war. But their contribution to securing the turning point did allow them to sleep in their beds—and enabled the readers of these pages to sleep in peace.

- Commando training centres, 1941-1943
- Commando training centres in the six months before D-Day

SCOTLAND

Achnacarry
▲ *Ben Nevis*
Inveraray
Helensburgh
Largs
Troon
Whiting Bay
Girvan

North Sea

North Channel

NORTHERN IRELAND

Strangford Lough

Irish Sea

Featherstonehaugh

Ringway

Criccieth   Wrexham

St. George's Channel

ENGLAND

WALES

Brightlingsea

Theale   Pinner
                Gravesend   Herne Bay
                         Canterbury   Ramsgate
                         Folkestone   Dover

Bristol Channel

Coldhayes   Littlehampton
Warsash   Hove   Hastings
Lee on Solent   Worthing   Bexhill
                       South   Eastbourne
Paignton   Weymouth   Hayling   Seaford
                              Southsea

St Ives   Dartmouth

Falmouth

English Channel

FRANCE

kilometres 100
miles 60

© Sir Martin Gilbert 2003

1. Commando training bases.

182

2. Landing craft building yards in the United States.

3. Amphibious landing training sites.

4. "Big Week" bombing raids, 20–26 February 1944.

North
Sea

GREAT
●Fulbeck
A DIVISION

The Wash

East Dereham
A DIVISION
●

Beccles
STAFF HEADQUARTERS
OF AN INFANTRY DIVISION
●

Leicester●
A DIVISION

BRITAIN

Bury St Edmunds
A DIVISION
●

Newmarket
A DIVISION
(Belgian)

Woodbridge
A DIVISION
●

Ipswich ●
A DIVISION

River Thames

●Bristol
AN ARMY CORPS

Sunningdale ●
AN ARMY GROUP

Gravesend ●
A DIVISION

Canterbury A DIVISION
●

Bulford ●
AN ARMY CORPS

Three Bridges
A DIVISION ●

Tunbridge Wells
● AN ARMY
CORPS

Folkestone
AN ARMY
CORPS

Heathfield AN ARMY ●

Hailsham A BRIGADE ●

PAS-DE-CALAIS

English Channel

FRANCE

0   kilometres   50

0   miles   30

NORMANDY

© Sir Martin Gilbert 2003

5. German Intelligence assessment of the location of the "bogus" First United States Army Group (FUSAG).

FIRST NORWEGIAN ARMY

UNIDENTIFIED NORWEGIAN BRIGADE

Inverness

UNIDENTIFIED BRITISH DIVISION

Aberdeen

12th NORWEGIAN INFANTRY BRIGADE

S C O T L A N D

VII ARMY CORPS (BRITISH)

55th MOTORIZED INFANTRY DIVISION (AMERICAN)

52nd MOTORIZED INFANTRY DIVISION (BRITISH)

North Sea

2nd POLISH INFANTRY DIVISION

HEADQUARTERS, SCOTTISH ARMY

Perth

POLISH PARACHUTE BRIGADE

2nd POLISH INFANTRY DIVISION

Fife Ness

FIRST ARMY CORPS (BRITISH)

FIRST ARMY CORP (Polish)

Firth of Forth

AMERICAN INFANTRY DIVISION

Clyde

Glasgow

Edinburgh

1st POLISH ARMOURED DIVISION

50th MOTORIZED INFANTRY DIVISION

58th MOTORIZED INFANTRY DIVISION

© Sir Martin Gilbert 2003

● British troops   ◖ Norwegian troops
○ Polish troops   ◉ American troops

6. German Intelligence assessment of the "bogus" Allied army in Scotland, 15 May 1944.

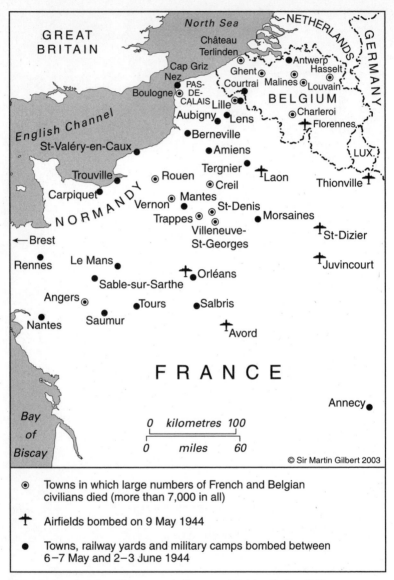

GREAT
BRITAIN

North Sea

Château
Terlinden

Cap Griz
Nez
PAS-
Boulogne ◉ DE-
CALAIS

Antwerp
Hasselt
Ghent ◉
Courtrai
Malines ◉ Louvain
BELGIUM
Lille ◉
Aubigny
Lens
Charleroi ◉
✝ Florennes

English Channel

St-Valéry-en-Caux
Berneville
Amiens

LUX.

Trouville
◉ Rouen
Tergnier
✝ Laon
Thionville ✝

Carpiquet
◉ Creil
◉ Mantes
Vernon ◉ St-Denis
Morsaines
NORMANDY
Trappes ◉ ◉
Villeneuve-
St-Georges ◉
✈ St-Dizier

← Brest

Le Mans
✝ Orléans
✈ Juvincourt

Rennes

Sable-sur-Sarthe
Angers ◉
Tours
Salbris
Nantes
Saumur
✝ Avord

F R A N C E

Annecy ●

*Bay
of
Biscay*

| 0 | kilometres | 100 |
| 0 | miles | 60 |

© Sir Martin Gilbert 2003

◉   Towns in which large numbers of French and Belgian
      civilians died (more than 7,000 in all)

✝   Airfields bombed on 9 May 1944

●   Towns, railway yards and military camps bombed between
      6–7 May and 2–3 June 1944

7. Anglo-American bombing targets in France and Belgium before D-Day.

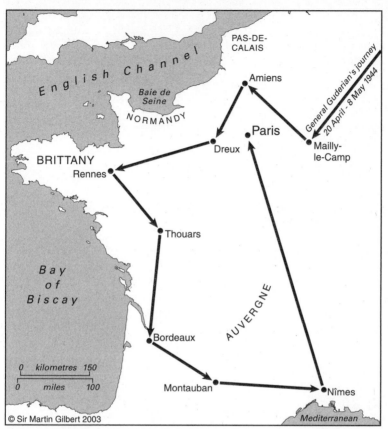

8. General Guderian's journey, 20 April to 8 May 1944.

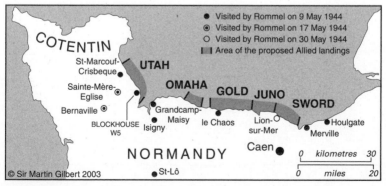

9. Field Marshal Rommel's tours of inspection in the month before D-Day.

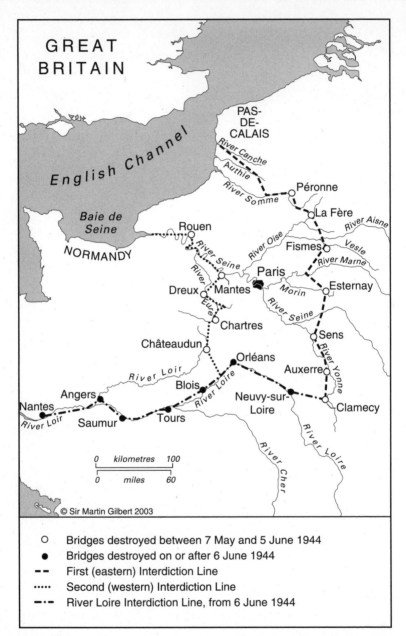

GREAT
BRITAIN

PAS-
DE-
CALAIS

River Canche

Authie

River Somme

Péronne

La Fère

River Aisne

River Oise

Fismes

Vesle

River Marne

Paris

Esternay

Morin

River Seine

Sens

River Yonne

English Channel

Baie de Seine

NORMANDY

Rouen

River Seine

River

Dreux

Mantes

Eure

Chartres

Châteaudun

Orléans

Blois

River Loire

Neuvy-sur-Loire

Auxerre

Clamecy

River Loir

Angers

Nantes

River Loir

Saumur

Tours

River Loire

River Cher

River Loire

0	kilometres	100
0	miles	60

© Sir Martin Gilbert 2003

○   Bridges destroyed between 7 May and 5 June 1944

●   Bridges destroyed on or after 6 June 1944

– –   First (eastern) Interdiction Line

·····   Second (western) Interdiction Line

–·–   River Loire Interdiction Line, from 6 June 1944

10. The Anglo-American bombing campaign against the river bridges, 7 May to 6 June 1944.

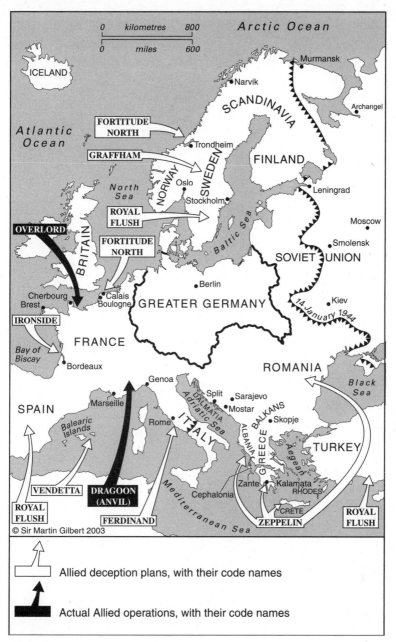

11. Anglo-American plans and deception plans.

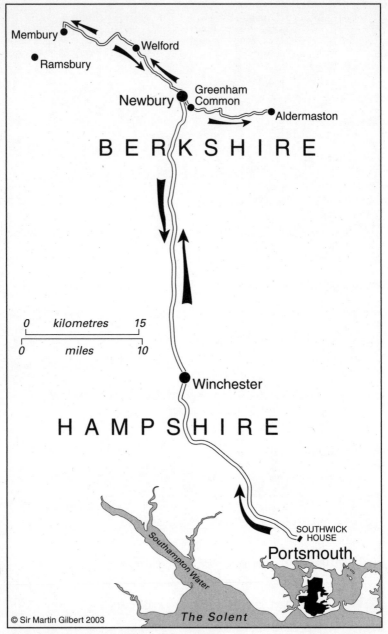

Membury
Ramsbury
Welford
Newbury
Greenham Common
Aldermaston

B E R K S H I R E

0 kilometres 15
0 miles 10

Winchester

H A M P S H I R E

Southampton Water

SOUTHWICK
HOUSE

Portsmouth

The Solent

© Sir Martin Gilbert 2003

12. General Eisenhower's journey, 5 June 1944.

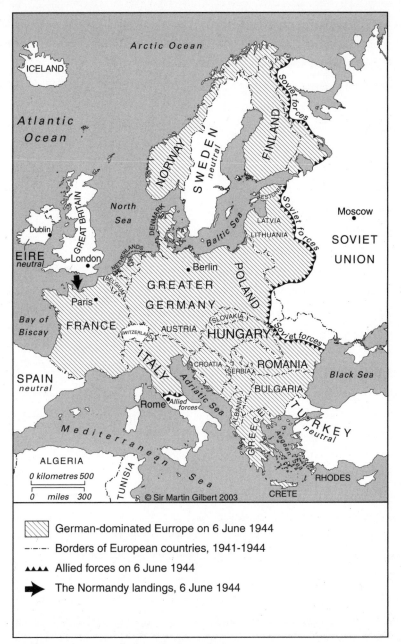

13. German-dominated Europe on 6 June 1944.

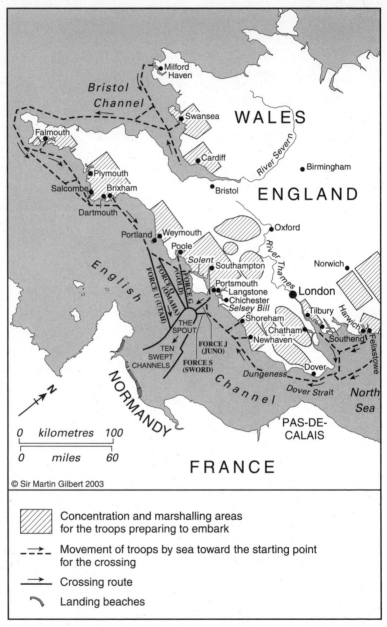

14. Troop concentrations in Britain and the movement by sea toward Normandy, 1–6 June 1944.

The American air forces shown on this map constituted almost half of the total force in action, and the most easterly assembly area, during the early hours of 6 June 1944

o Air bases
- -→ Flight paths

North Sea

Harrogate
York
Preston
Beverley
Bawtry
Runcorn

GREAT
BRITAIN

Wolverhampton
Swaffham
Worcester
Thetford
Bedford
Bassingbourn
Bicester
Debden
Cheltenham
London
Swindon
Dartford
Newbury
Gillingham
Gravesend
Thames Estuary
Taunton
Winchester
Dover Strait
PAS-DE-CALAIS
Selsey Bill
Worthing
Littlehampton
Brighton
Newhaven
Beachy Head
ISLE OF WIGHT
Severn

English Channel

0 kilometres 50
0 miles 30

FRANCE

Baie de Seine

NORMANDY

© Sir Martin Gilbert 2003

15. United States Army Air Force assembly and flight paths on the eve of the Normandy landings.

195

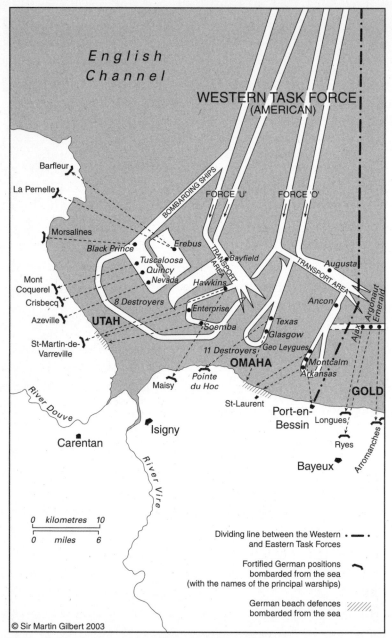

English Channel

WESTERN TASK FORCE
(AMERICAN)

Barfleur

La Pernelle

FORCE 'U' FORCE 'O'

Morsalines

Erebus

Black Prince

Tuscaloosa

Quincy

Nevada

Mont Coquerel

Crisbecq

Azeville

8 Destroyers

Hawkins

Bayfield

Augusta

Ancon

Enterprise

Soemba

Texas

Glasgow

Geo Leygues

Ajax

Argonaut

Emerald

UTAH

St-Martin-de-Varreville

11 Destroyers

OMAHA

Montcalm

Arkansas

GOLD

River Douve

Maisy

Pointe du Hoc

St-Laurent

Port-en-Bessin

Longues

Ryes

Isigny

Carentan

River Vire

Bayeux

Aromanches

| 0 | kilometres | 10 |
| 0 | miles | 6 |

Dividing line between the Western and Eastern Task Forces —·—·

Fortified German positions bombarded from the sea (with the names of the principal warships)

German beach defences bombarded from the sea ////

© Sir Martin Gilbert 2003

16. Naval forces in action, 6 June 1944: the Western Task Force.

196

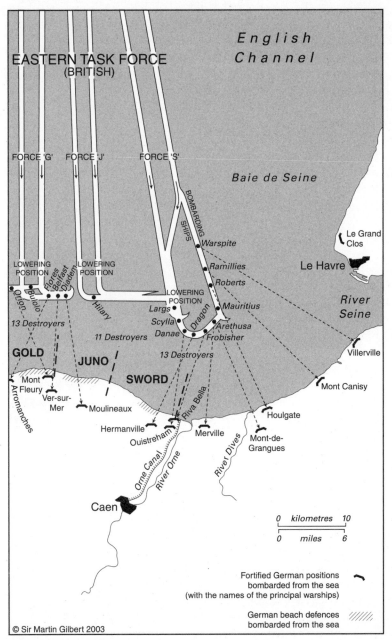

17. Naval forces in action, 6 June 1944: the Eastern Task Force.

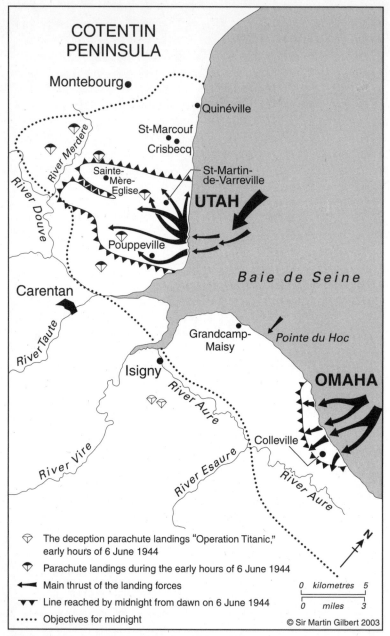

COTENTIN PENINSULA

Montebourg

Quinéville

St-Marcouf

Crisbecq

Sainte-Mère-Eglise

St-Martin-de-Varreville

UTAH

Pouppeville

River Merdère

River Douve

Baie de Seine

Carentan

River Taute

Grandcamp-Maisy

Pointe du Hoc

Isigny

River Aure

OMAHA

Colleville

River Vire

River Esaure

River Aure

⬦ The deception parachute landings "Operation Titanic," early hours of 6 June 1944

◈ Parachute landings during the early hours of 6 June 1944

◄ Main thrust of the landing forces

▼▼ Line reached by midnight from dawn on 6 June 1944

•••• Objectives for midnight

N

| 0 | kilometres | 5 |
| 0 | miles | 3 |

© Sir Martin Gilbert 2003

18. The Utah and Omaha Beach landings, 6 June 1944.

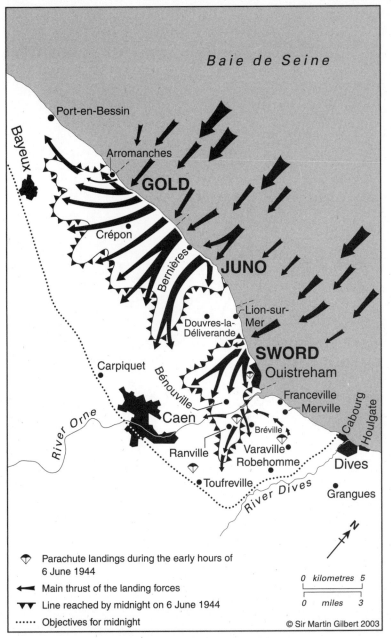

Baie de Seine

Port-en-Bessin
Bayeux
Arromanches
GOLD
Crépon
Bernières
JUNO
Lion-sur-Mer
Douvres-la-Délliverande
SWORD
Carpiquet
Ouistreham
Bénouville
Franceville
Merville
River Orne
Caen
Bréville
Ranville
Varaville
Robehomme
Toufreville
Grangues
River Dives
Cabourg
Houlgate
Dives
N

⬙ Parachute landings during the early hours of
  6 June 1944

◄━ Main thrust of the landing forces

▼▼ Line reached by midnight on 6 June 1944

••••• Objectives for midnight

| 0 | kilometres | 5 |
| 0 | miles | 3 |

© Sir Martin Gilbert 2003

19. The Gold, Juno, and Sword Beach landings, 6 June 1944.

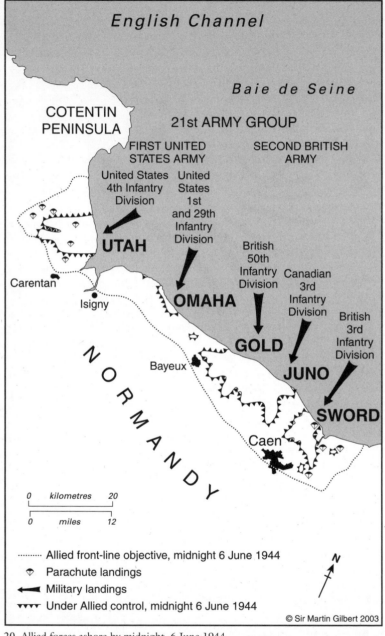

20. Allied forces ashore by midnight, 6 June 1944.

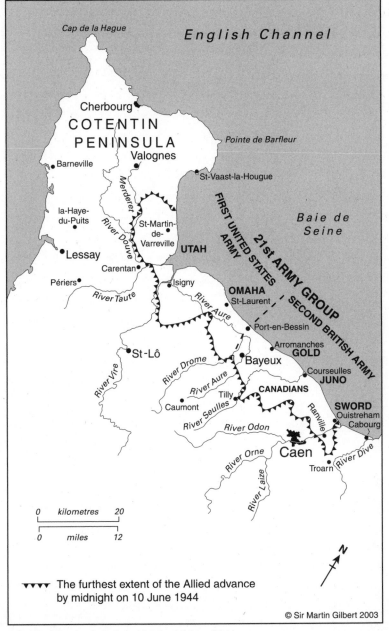

Cap de la Hague

English Channel

Cherbourg

COTENTIN
PENINSULA

Pointe de Barfleur

Valognes

Barneville

St-Vaast-la-Hougue

*Baie de
Seine*

la-Haye-
du-Puits

St-Martin-
de-
Varreville

River Merderet

River Douve

UTAH

Lessay

Carentan

Périers

Isigny

River Taute

River Aure

OMAHA
St-Laurent

FIRST UNITED STATES ARMY

21st ARMY GROUP / SECOND BRITISH ARMY

Port-en-Bessin

St-Lô

River Vire

River Drome

River Aure

Arromanches

GOLD

Bayeux

Courseulles

JUNO

Tilly

Caumont

River Seulles

CANADIANS

SWORD
Ouistreham
Cabourg

River Odon

Ranville

Caen

River Orne

River Laize

Troarn

River Dive

N

0   kilometres   20

0   miles   12

▼▼▼▼ The furthest extent of the Allied advance
by midnight on 10 June 1944

© Sir Martin Gilbert 2003

21. Allied forces ashore by midnight, 10 June 1944.

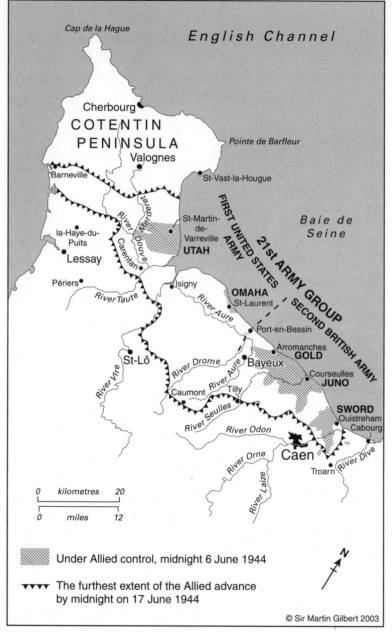

22. Allied forces ashore by midnight, 17 June 1944.

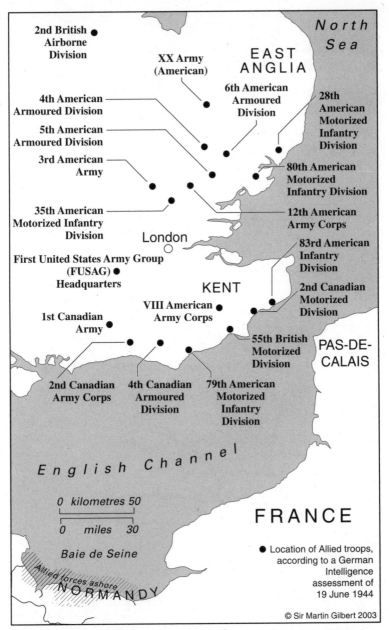

23. German Intelligence assessment of the location of the "bogus" First United States Army Group (FUSAG), 19 June 1944.

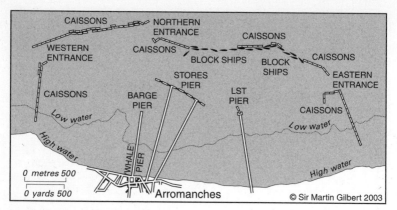

24. The Mulberry Harbor at Arromanches.

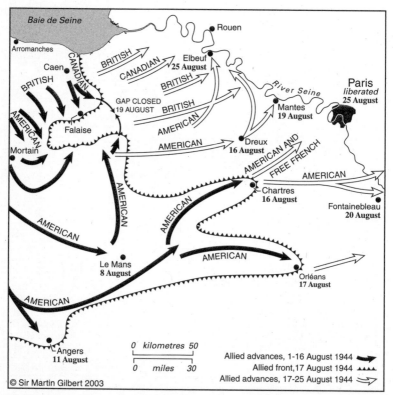

25. The Allied military advance, 1–25 August 1944.

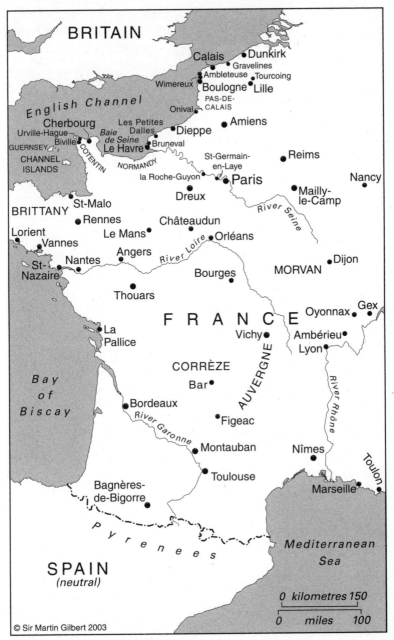

26. Places in France mentioned in this book.

27. Places in England mentioned in this book.

Bibliography of Works Consulted

Reference Works

Chandler, Edward G., and James Lawton Collins Jr. *The D-Day Encyclopedia*. New York: Simon & Schuster, 1994.

Dear, I. C. B., and M. R. D. Foot. *The Oxford Companion to World War II*. Oxford, Eng.: Oxford University Press, 1995.

Fuehrer Conferences on Naval Affairs, 1939–1945. London: Greenhill Books, 1990.

Holt, Tonie and Valmai. *Major and Mrs. Holt's Battlefield Guide to the Normandy Landing Beaches*, 2nd edition. Barnsley, South Yorkshire, Eng.: Leo Cooper, 2000.

Jordan, Kenneth N. Sr. *Yesterday's Heroes: 433 Men of World War II Awarded the Medal of Honor 1941–1945*. Atglen, Penn.: Schiffer Military History, 1966.

Middlebrook, Martin, and Chris Everitt. *The Bomber Command War Diaries: An Operational Reference Book, 1939–1945*. London: Penguin Books, 1990.

Ramsey, Winston G., ed. *D-Day Then and Now*, Two Volumes. London: Battle of Britain Prints International Ltd., 1995.

General Books

Barber, Neil. *The Day the Devils Dropped In: The 9th Parachute Battalion in Normandy, D-Day to D+6*. London: Leo Cooper, 2002.

Bennett, Ralph. *Ultra in the West: The Normandy Campaign of 1944–45*. London: Hutchinson, 1979.

Blandford, Edmund. *Two Sides of the Beach: The invasion and defence of Europe in 1944*. Shrewsbury, Eng.: Airlife, 1999.

Bradford, Sarah. *King George VI*. London: Weidenfeld & Nicolson, 1989.

Bradley, General Omar N. *A Soldier's Story*. London: Eyre & Spottiswoode, 1952.

Bryant, Arthur. *Triumph in the West*. London: Collins, 1959 (the diaries of Field Marshal Viscount Alanbrooke).

Budiansky, Stephen. *Air Power: From Kitty Hawk to Gulf War II: A History of the People, Ideas, and Machines That Transformed War in the Century of Flight*. London: Viking Penguin, 2003.

Chalfont, Alun. *Montgomery of Alamein*. London: Weidenfeld & Nicolson, 1976.

Chandler, A. D., ed. *The Papers of Dwight David Eisenhower*, Volume One. Baltimore: Johns Hopkins University Press, 1970.

Churchill, Winston S. *The Second World War*, Volume Five. London: Cassell, 1952.

Cookridge, E. H. *Inside SOE*. London: Arthur Barker, 1966.

Copp, Terry, and Robert Vogel. *Maple Leaf Route: Caen*. Alma, Ont.: Maple Leaf Route, 1983. The Canadian forces in Normandy.

Delve, Ken. *D-Day: The Air Battle*. London: Arms and Armour Press, 1984.

Dilks, David, ed. *The Diaries of Sir Alexander Cadogan, 1938–1945*. London: Cassell, 1971.

Eiler, Keith E., ed. *Wedemeyer on War and Peace*. Stanford, Calif.: Hoover Institution Press, 1987.

Eisenhower, Dwight D. *Crusade in Europe*. London: William Heinemann, 1948.

Ellis, Major L. F. *Victory in the West*. Volume I, *The Battle of Normandy*. London: Her Majesty's Stationery Office, 1962.

Foot, M. R. D. *SOE in France: An Account of the Work of the British Special Operations Executive in France 1940–1944*. London: Her Majesty's Stationery Office, 1966.

Fussell, Paul. *The Boys' Crusade: The American Infantry in North-western Europe, 1944–1945*. New York: Modern Library, 2003.

Gilbert, Martin. *Winston S. Churchill*. Volume Seven, *Road to Victory, 1941–1944*. London: William Heinemann, 1986.

Hastings, Max. *Das Reich: Resistance and the March of the 2nd SS Panzer Division through France, June 1944*. London: Michael Joseph, 1981.

Hinsley, F. H., and C. A. G. Simkins. *British Intelligence in the Second World War.* Volume Four, *Security and Counter-Intelligence.* London: Her Majesty's Stationery Office, 1990.

Hinsley, F. H., E. E. Thomas, G. F. G. Ransom, and R. C. Knight. *British Intelligence in the Second World War.* Volumes Two and Three. London: Her Majesty's Stationery Office, 1981–1988.

Howard, Michael. *British Intelligence in the Second World War.* Volume V, *Strategic Deception.* London: Her Majesty's Stationery Office, 1990.

Lord Ismay, *The Memoirs of General Lord Ismay.* London: Cassell, 1960.

Jones, R. V. *Reflections on Intelligence.* London: Heinemann, 1989.

Keegan, John. *Six Armies in Normandy: From D-Day to the Liberation of Paris.* London: Jonathan Cape, 1982.

Longmate, Norman. *The Doodlebugs: The Story of the Flying Bombs.* London: Hutchinson, 1981.

Macdermott, Brian. *Ships without Names: The Story of the Royal Navy's Tank Landing Ships of World War Two.* London: Arms and Armour Press, 1992.

McKee, Alexander. *Caen: Anvil of Victory.* London: Souvenir Press, 1964.

Messenger, Charles. *The Commandos, 1940–1956.* London: William Kimber, 1985.

Montgomery, Field Marshal Viscount of Alamein. *From Normandy to the Baltic.* London: Hutchinson, 1946.

Neillands, Robin. *The Battle of Normandy, 1944.* London: Cassell, 2002.

North, John. *North-West Europe, 1944–5: The Achievement of 21st Army Group.* London: Her Majesty's Stationery Office, 1953.

Ruby, Marcel. *F Section, SOE: The Buckmaster Networks.* London: Leo Cooper, 1988.

Saunders, Hilary St. George. *Royal Air Force, 1939–1945.* Volume Three, *The Fight Is Won.* London: Her Majesty's Stationery Office, 1954.

Thomas, David A. *The Atlantic Star, 1939–45.* London: W. H. Allen, 1990.

Warlimont, Walter. *Inside Hitler's Headquarters 1939–45.* London: Weidenfeld & Nicolson, 1965.

Articles

Fowlie, Jonathan. "Veterans Recall Longest Day." Toronto *Globe and Mail,* June 6, 2003.

Shmulewitz, Y. "The Rescue of 15 Jews in the Attic of a Pigsty." (In Yiddish.) *Forward* (New York), June 27, 1964.

Thompson, R. W. "Build-Up for D-Day: Embattled Island." Article 1796, *History of the Second World War.* London: Purnell, 1967.

Willans, Major T. W. "The Bruneval Raid." Article 853, *History of the Second World War.* London: Purnell, 1967.

Young, Brigadier Peter. "The First Commando raids." Article 841, *History of the Second World War.* London: Purnell, 1967.

Obituaries

"Major-General B. P. Hughes: Montgomery's anti aircraft adviser." *The Times* (London), 12 September 1989.

"Michel Pichard." *The Times* (London), 23 September 1989.

"Lord Cheshire, VC, OM." *The Times* (London), 3 August 1992.

"Canon David Strangeways." *The Times* (London), 5 August 1998.

"Major John Howard." *The Times* (London), 7 May 1999.

"Rear-Admiral Colin Madden." *The Times* (London), 5 July 2000.

"Group Captain Hugh Verity." *The Times* (London), 19 November 2001.

"Lieutenant-Colonel Johnny Cooper." *The Times* (London), 13 July 2002.

"His Honour D. A. Grant" ["Tommy" Grant]. *The Times* (London), 13 September 2002.

"Captain Robert Lloyd." *The Times* (London), 21 March 2003.

"Doon Campbell: Reuters Reporter." *Independent,* 7 August 2003.

"Ex-Politician and War Hero Flynn Dies" [Dennis Flynn]. *Globe and Mail,* (Toronto) 20 August 2003.

Index

Page numbers followed by *n* are footnotes.